Unlocking the Bible

Cultural Keys to Understanding the Scriptures

By
Yesu Vi

Copyright 2024 Well-Being Publishing. All rights reserved.

No part of this book may be reproduced in any form or by any electronic or mechanical means including information storage and retrieval systems, without permission in writing from the author. The only exception is by a reviewer, who may quote short excerpts in a review.

Although the author and publisher have made every effort to ensure that the information in this book was correct at press time, the author and publisher do not assume and hereby disclaim any liability to any party for any loss, damage, or disruption caused by errors or omissions, whether such errors or omissions result from negligence, accident, or any other cause.

This publication is designed to provide accurate and authoritative information with regard to the subject matter covered. It is sold with the understanding that the publisher is not engaged in rendering professional services. If legal advice or other expert assistance is required, the services of a competent professional should be sought.

The fact that an organization or website is referred to in this work as a citation and/or a potential source of further information does not mean that the author or the publisher endorses the information the organization or website may provide or recommendations it may make.

Please remember that Internet websites listed in this work may have changed or disappeared between when this work was written and when it is read.

To you,
Thank you!

Table of Contents

Introduction 1

Chapter 1: Understanding the Context of the Bible 4
    Cultural Contexts of the Bible 4
    Historical Contexts of the Bible 8

Chapter 2: The Language of the Scriptures 12
    Original Languages of the Bible 12
    Translation Challenges and Triumphs 19

Chapter 3: The Cultural World of Genesis 22
    Social Structures in Genesis 23
    Theological Themes in Genesis 25

Chapter 4: Exodus and the Birth of a Nation 29
    Cultural Influences in Exodus 29
    Theological Implications of the Exodus 33

Chapter 5: Kings and Prophets 37
    The Monarchical Period 37
    The Role of Prophets in Israelite Culture 41

Chapter 6: Wisdom Literature 44
    Cultural Insights from Proverbs 44
    Ecclesiastes and the Search for Meaning 48

Chapter 7: The Influence of the Babylonian Exile 52
    Life in Exile 53
    Cultural and Religious Adaptations During Exile 55

Chapter 8: Intertestamental Developments 59
    Hellenistic Influence on Jewish Culture 59
    Significance of the Dead Sea Scrolls 63

Chapter 9: The Cultural Background of the Gospels 66
    Jewish Life in the First Century 67
    Roman Impact on Judea 70

Chapter 10: Acts and the Early Church 74
    Cultural Expansion of Christianity 74
    Theological Foundations in Acts 78

Chapter 11: Pauline Epistles and Cultural Engagement 82
    Paul's Cultural Contexts 83
    Key Themes in the Epistles 86

Chapter 12: Revelation and Apocalyptic Literature 90
    Cultural and Historical Context of Revelation 91
    Interpretation Challenges and Cultural Insights 94

Conclusion 95

Appendix A: Appendix 98
    Additional Resources for Cultural and Historical
    Studies of the Bible 98

Introduction

The Bible stands as one of the most influential texts in human history. Its vast tapestry weaves together stories, teachings, and parables that have shaped the spiritual, cultural, and ethical foundations of societies for over two millennia. But to truly engage with its profound wisdom, one must first embark on a journey to understand the world in which these texts were written. This exploration of context not only enriches our understanding but also deepens our relationship with the Scriptures.

Consider this endeavor as peeling back layers of time. Imagine standing at the crossroads where ancient traditions meet divine inspiration, where the echoes of past civilizations resonate through the canon of biblical literature. The Bible isn't just a collection of isolated writings; it's a living document that has traveled through time, through cultural and historical landscapes that influence its narratives. Each verse and chapter is imbued with the spirit and essence of the age and region from which it emerged.

Many readers approach the Bible seeking solace, guidance, or understanding, all of which are noble pursuits. Yet, to glean the most profound insights, it's essential to appreciate the nuances of its context. Just as a gem reveals its utmost brilliance when observed from multiple angles, so too does Scripture when viewed through the lens of its environment. By understanding the cultural, historical, and linguistic facets, we derive a richer comprehension and appreciation of its message.

As we proceed to explore these contexts, we'll find that the Bible was written by people steeped in the customs and mindsets of their times. For instance, the rich cultural traditions of the Near East, the sociopolitical dynamics of the Roman Empire, and the spiritual journeys of the Israelites all color the narratives. These are not mere background details; they are integral to the message and meaning of the Scriptures.

The Bible's cultural tapestry is as varied as it is vast. From the patriarchal families of Genesis, reflecting ancient kinship structures, to the sophisticated debates of Job and Ecclesiastes, which mirror the existential ponderings relevant then and now, the Scriptures invite us to delve deeper. These writings speak to the heart of human experiences, transcending mere historical accounts to touch upon eternal truths and insights into humanity's relationship with the divine.

Then there's the intriguing quest of language. The Scriptures are primarily composed in Hebrew, Greek, and a smattering of Aramaic—each language bearing its unique idiomatic expressions and literary styles that still engage scholars and theologians with new interpretations today. Consider, too, the monumental efforts and challenges of translating these texts through the ages, aiming to preserve their original intent while making them accessible to a broader audience, as seen in the respected translation of the King James Version.

As this book unfolds, we aim to guide you through biblical history and culture, shedding light on the myriad influences at play. You'll uncover how the significance of the Exodus transcends mere liberation to become a metaphor for spiritual awakening and freedom. You'll journey through the wisdom literature of Proverbs, offering glimpses into ancient life's rhythm, ethos, and values, echoing truths that remain relevant in our modern world.

Unlocking the Bible

We invite you to open your heart and mind to the profound depths of these sacred texts, encouraging you to view them not just as historical documents but as living stories with the power to transform and inspire. In the words of the apostle Paul, "For whatsoever things were written aforetime were written for our learning, that we through patience and comfort of the scriptures might have hope" (Romans. 15:4). This hope, nurtured by understanding, is the gift we hope to offer through this exploration.

Let this book serve as a guide and companion as you embark on this journey. It invites both new believers and seasoned scholars alike to approach the Scriptures with fresh eyes and open hearts, to rediscover the beauty and depth of a text that has, and continues to, shape the course of history. Together, we aspire to connect with the timeless truths of the Bible, bridging the past with the present and lighting the path for the future. With each chapter, may you find renewed inspiration, perspective, and wisdom.

Chapter 1: Understanding the Context of the Bible

Diving into the Scriptures, it's essential to recognize that the Bible wasn't written in a vacuum, but within rich, complex cultural and historical tapestries. Each book is a reflection of the times and settings in which it was crafted. Understanding these contexts is not just an academic exercise; it's a transformational journey that illuminates the wisdom held within these sacred texts. Think of the Bible as a mosaic, each piece representing not only divine inspiration but also the unique influences of the surrounding society. From the laws of ancient Israel to the teachings of Jesus, knowing the backdrop of these events can profoundly deepen our comprehension and spiritual journey. For instance, when Jesus states, "Ye are the light of the world. A city that is set on a hill cannot be hid" (Matthew. 5:14), we grasp its full significance by appreciating its cultural references and the expectations of His audience. By examining the Bible through these lenses, we open our hearts and minds to a fuller understanding of its messages and apply them more precisely in our lives today.

Cultural Contexts of the Bible

The cultural landscape of the biblical world is a rich tapestry woven with diverse practices, beliefs, and societal norms that shape the narratives and teachings within the Scriptures. From the patriarchal traditions of the early Israelites to the Greco-Roman influences in the time of the New Testament, understanding these cultural contexts deepens our reading of the Bible. Each book of the Bible was written not in isolation but amidst a specific cultural milieu, reflecting and sometimes challenging the societal norms of its time. For instance, the practice of hospitality in ancient Near Eastern culture turns a simple story into a profound lesson, as seen when Abraham entertains angels unawares. "Be not forgetful to entertain strangers: for thereby some have entertained angels unawares" (Hebrews. 13:2). This cultural lens helps us see the Scriptures not just as ancient texts but as living documents inviting us to consider how ancient truths still resonate today. It's in these layers of cultural context that we find inspiration for our journeys, seeing how faith transcends time, yet is deeply rooted in the human experience. The richness of the biblical world beckons us to explore deeper, to seek understanding, and ultimately, to let these ancient stories illuminate the pathways of our own lives.

Importance of the Cultural Context ... Understanding the Bible without grasping the cultural milieu in which it was written is akin to wandering through a bustling city blindfolded. The words of Scripture were spoken and transcribed in specific settings, among particular peoples, and within unique social constructs. These are not mere relics of the past, but vital keys that unlock deeper comprehensions of biblical texts. By revealing the cultural essence, we not only navigate these ancient streets with confidence, but we also discover the vibrant life that pulsates through them.

The Bible unfolds across diverse cultures and societies, each wrestling with its own array of beliefs, customs, and social hierarchies. Recognizing these cultural layers enriches our understanding of God's message. Consider how the Israelites, wandering through the wilderness, were shaped by their previous bondage in Egypt. Their laws, traditions, and visions of justice were deeply intertwined with that cultural memory. A commandment such as "Thou shalt not oppress a stranger: for ye know the heart of a stranger, seeing ye were strangers in the land of Egypt" (Exodus. 23:9) becomes much more profound when viewed through this lens.

Drifting into the poetic verses of Psalms, or the wise maxims of Proverbs, one may stumble if unaware of the cultural ingredients that flavored their creation. Hebrew poetry, for instance, makes abundant use of parallelism—a literary form popular in the ancient Near East. A clear grasp of this stylistic choice can transform reading from a mere recitation into an insightful reflection that resonates today. Similarly, the book of Proverbs offers an anthology of insights deeply rooted in the day-to-day life of ancient Israelite society. When one perceives these maxims in the cultural context of family and community-centered living, their applicability magnifies.

The importance of cultural context becomes even more pronounced when engaging with the narratives of the New Testament. Jesus' parables, often taught in the fields or along the bustling roads of first-century Judea, brim with cultural references familiar to his listeners. Understanding this context transforms parables from enigmatic stories to powerfully persuasive teachings. Take, for instance, the parable of the Good Samaritan. Without appreciating the societal animosity between Jews and Samaritans, the act of a Samaritan helping a wounded Jew can seem merely charitable, rather than groundbreaking and scandalous for its time.

Additionally, Paul's epistles overflow with cultural nuances. Paul, a Jew born in a Hellenistic society, understood the critical importance of cultural adaptation to spread the Gospel effectively. "For though I be free from all men, yet have I made myself servant unto all, that I might gain the more" (1 Corinthians. 9:19). Here, Paul's words reveal a strategic adaptation to cultural contexts to foster relatability and open pathways for dialogue, demonstrating a thoughtful engagement with varying cultural frameworks.

It's also imperative to think about the cultural backdrop when interpreting prophetic literature. The prophets of Israel communicated not only in challenging times but also under the pressure of looming empires and shifting allegiances. Grasping the political and cultural landscapes, such as the Assyrian threat during Isaiah's ministry or the Babylonian exile impacting Ezekiel and Daniel, provides crucial clarity to their messages of hope and warning.

When looking at wisdom literature and profound books like Job or Ecclesiastes, cultural perspectives offer further insights. Job's story, with its ancient questions of suffering and justice, reflects a universal quest that transcends time, yet emerges from a milieu rich in its own existential wrestling. Similarly, Ecclesiastes provides vibrant philosophical reflections on life's meaning, echoing an ancient worldview still relevant in today's search for purpose.

Furthermore, considering the cultural and historical context of Revelation enables us to approach its apocalyptic visions with greater wisdom. A work saturated with imagery and symbolism commonplace in its time, yet baffling today, demands an understanding of its cultural origins to be comprehensible and inspirational.

As we deepen our study into the cultural contexts of the Bible, it's important to remember that we are not merely embarking on an academic quest. We are engaging with a living document meant to transform lives. It takes mindfulness to allow these cultural insights to deepen our spiritual journey, enhancing our faith and practice. With each layer uncovered, fresh perspectives unfold, inviting us to walk not just alongside historical communities but in the presence of a timeless, divine guidance.

Embrace this journey as a extraordinary voyage, one that embraces the cultural Earth beneath your feet, for in doing so, the weight and wisdom of Scripture become all the more substantial and illuminating. Whether reading the oft-quoted maxims of Proverbs, the heartfelt letters of Paul, or the revelatory visions of John, understanding the cultural context is not simply beneficial; it is transformative, lifting the biblical narrative from the past into our present, where its truths continue to uplift and inspire.

Historical Contexts of the Bible

In unraveling the historical contexts of the Bible, we must journey back to the ancient era where empires rose and fell, each leaving an indelible mark on the landscape of biblical narrative. The Scriptures were birthed in a world teeming with tumult and transformation, capturing the echoes of events such as the ascension of Babylon and Persia, the Greek conquests, and the dominion of Rome. These historical backdrops are not mere settings; they are silent guides that shape and illuminate the meaning of biblical events and prophecies. By examining these past events, we see how God interacted with humanity, manifesting His divine will amidst the ebbs and flows of human history. The Old Testament, with its tales of Exodus and Exile, and the New Testament, in the shadow of Roman might, each bring a textured understanding of how the threads of divine purpose were woven throughout disparate epochs. As Paul wrote, "All things work together for good to them that love God" (Romans. 8:28), underscoring that even amid historical upheaval, God's eternal plan moves ever forward. Engaging with this historical tapestry, we not only deepen our comprehension of the Scriptures but also ignite a transformative appreciation for the persistence of faith across the treadmill of time.

Key Historical Events Impacting the Scriptures are a constellation of significant occurrences that navigated the course of biblical history, providing invaluable context for understanding the sacred texts. From ancient conquests to cataclysmic exiles, these events are the sinews connecting the flesh and bones of biblical narratives. In considering these events, we appreciate how they shaped not only the history of a people but also the theological content and direction of the Scriptures themselves. Every event, like a master key, unlocks facets of the Scriptures that might otherwise remain obscured to modern eyes.

One finds that the exodus from Egypt is one of the earliest and most defining events of biblical history. It's more than the escape of a people from slavery; it's a formative moment for the Israelites, forever branding their identity as a chosen people liberated by the divine hand of God. "And the LORD said unto Moses, Wherefore criest thou unto me? Speak unto the children of Israel, that they go forward" (Exodus. 14:15). This event resonates throughout the entire biblical corpus, symbolizing redemption, teaching trust in divine providence, and establishing the law. Without this key event, many other narratives would lack their foundational backstory.

When we leap into the era of monarchies, the establishment of the Kingdom of Israel stands as a watershed moment. Under Saul, David, and Solomon, Israel not only found territorial expansion but also spiritual consolidation. The Davidic Covenant assured the Israelites of perpetual divine support, framing the theological backdrop against which much of prophecy and messianic expectation unraveled. David's reign also marked a period where psalms and prayers took literary form, enriching the devotional and worship framework of future generations. Imagine how different the tone of biblical prophecy and wisdom literature might be without the establishment of a monarchy.

The Babylonian exile, however, casts the longest shadow over the entire biblical narrative. This period of profound suffering and displacement punctuated an end to national sovereignty but opened a chapter of introspection and religious evolution. It was during this exile that much of the Old Testament content, including history and prophecy, found its final form. Jeremiah's warnings and Ezekiel's visions reflect the trauma and hope of a displaced people longing for return, as is encapsulated in the hopeful yet somber promise: "For I know the thoughts that I think towards you, saith the LORD, thoughts of peace, and not of evil, to give you an expected end" (Jeremiah. 29:11).

During the exile, Judaism evolved from its temple-centric practices to a more scripture- and synagogue-focused faith, setting the stage for post-exilic religious identity and practice. The compilation and canonization of scriptural texts gained urgency, providing solace and identity for a scattered people. What emerged was a renewal of theological reflection, nuanced by suffering yet vibrant with hope, preparing hearts for the eventual return from exile.

The intertestamental period, often glossed over, significantly impacted later Jewish thought and the context of the New Testament. Following the return from Babylon, Judea found itself under the shifting control of empires—first Persia, then Greece, and finally Rome. Each power influenced the culture and religious thought of the region differently. The Hellenistic influence, for example, introduced philosophies that challenged traditional Jewish thought, fostering the rise of groups like the Pharisees, Sadducees, and Essenes, each with distinctive interpretations of the Law. This era also saw the creation of the Septuagint, the Greek translation of Hebrew Scriptures, which would become essential for early Christian theology.

The life and ministry of Jesus Christ entered this complex cultural matrix, profoundly redefining the spiritual landscape. The Roman occupation of Judea set the stage for a socio-political climate ripe for messianic expectation. Jesus' teachings, rooted deeply in Jewish traditions yet revolutionary, addressed these anticipations uniquely. His life, death, and resurrection would later be interpreted as the ultimate pivot in human and divine history, prompting the rapid expansion of the Christian faith in a Greco-Roman world open to new ideas. His words, "Love thy neighbor as thyself," (Matthew. 22:39) came to represent a transformative ethic amidst political oppression.

The development and spread of early Christianity vividly illustrate the echoes of historical events in scrip-tural contexts. The destruction of the Second Temple in AD 70 marked a crucial moment for both Judaism and Christianity. For the Jewish community, it necessitated further theological and religious transformation without a centralized place of worship. For Christians, it reinforced Jesus' prophecies about the temple's destruction and helped delineate Christian identity further from Jewish roots. This period catalyzed the spread of Christianity beyond Judea's borders into the wider Roman Empire, spurred on by the apostles, including Paul, whose letters laid the theological and practical groundwork for burgeoning Christian communities.

Understanding these key historical events is like deciphering the DNA of the Scriptures; it illuminates the motivations, struggles, and ethos of the people at the heart of these texts. Just as a river is shaped by its contours and tributaries, Scripture is informed by the history it traverses. Appreciating these impact events offers readers more than historical curiosity—it opens avenues for spiritual enrichment, providing lessons on human resilience, divine faithfulness, and the perpetual hope woven into the narrative of God interacting with humanity. Through these events, one can perceive not only the past's imprint but also a present invitation to engage with Scripture as a living testament to transformation and faith.

Chapter 2:
The Language of the Scriptures

Unlocking the language of the scriptures is like discovering a sacred bridge stretching across time, connecting us to the divine narratives that have captivated hearts for millennia. The Bible speaks through a tapestry woven with the threads of Hebrew, Aramaic, and Greek, each adding unique hues to its profound messages. As we explore these original languages, we delve deeper into the essence of the sacred texts, where words like "In the beginning God created the heaven and the earth" (Genesis. 1:1) echo their ancient resonance. The challenges and triumphs of translating these scriptures over centuries have gifted us with versions that seek to maintain their spiritual core while navigating intricate linguistic shifts. This journey through words is not merely an academic exercise; it is a transformative path that echoes the eternal call to wisdom, understanding, and growth. As we engage with this linguistic heritage, we uncover new dimensions of meaning, reminding us that the scriptures are alive—dynamic vessels of divine truth, meant to inspire and guide every generation anew.

Original Languages of the Bible

The profound tapestry of the Bible unfolds through the original languages in which it was written—Hebrew, Aramaic, and Greek. These languages carry the essence of divine communication, weaving historical narratives, prophetic declarations, and timeless wisdom. Hebrew, the early voice of the Old Testament, echoes in the sacred texts with its poetic cadence and depth, unlocking the ancient paths of the Israelites as they journeyed with God. Aramaic, a language of transition and dissemination, bridges epochs and peoples, finding its heart in certain books and remembered in the words of Jesus on the cross: "Eli, Eli, lama sabachthani?"—an expression of profound anguish and fulfillment (Matthew. 27:46). Greek, the language of the New Testament, extends the reach of the gospel with clarity and philosophical precision, embodying the mission to spread the Good News to all nations. In unraveling these languages, we not only peel back layers of meaning but also draw closer to the divine intent, empowering us to navigate Scripture's profound mysteries with fresh perspectives and a renewed spirit.

Hebrew and Aramaic Texts delve into the very heart of the Scriptures, opening a window into ancient worlds where sacred words first took form. To truly embrace the resonance of these texts, one must set foot in the rich soil of their linguistic origins. Hebrew, the unyielding tongue of the Old Testament, is woven through the fabric of Israel's history and culture.

The Hebrew language is not merely a vehicle of communication but a vessel holding the pulse of an entire people. Its consonant-driven structure reverberates with a rhythm that mirrors the dynamic narrative of the Hebrew Bible. In Genesis, the breath of God moving across the waters is captured in sparse, poetic terms—a testament to the language's capacity for depth through simplicity: "In the beginning God created the heaven and the earth" (Genesis. 1:1). Such passages illuminate the powerful economy of Hebrew, where every letter is alive with potential meaning.

Scholars have long marveled at the linguistic precision of Hebrew, especially in the Ten Commandments, where each word is carefully chosen to convey moral imperatives that have stood the test of time. The language acts as a guardian of tradition, binding audiences of diverse eras to the core tenets of faith. Through Hebrew, timeless stories like that of Abraham and Isaac echo across generations, compelling readers to ponder the subtleties of faith and obedience.

Aramaic, while perhaps less well-known to some students of the Bible, also occupies a significant place in the Scriptures. It was the lingua franca of the Near East for centuries, soothing the rough edges of cultural exchange and enabling the words of prophets and visionaries to reach across ethnic and linguistic borders. Daniel and Ezra, among others, include significant portions written in this language.

The Aramaic texts within the Bible echo a period of transition and adaptation. For instance, when King Nebuchadnezzar calls upon Daniel to interpret dreams in his court, the narrative shifts fluidly from Hebrew to Aramaic, signifying broader dialogues in changing empires. By engaging with these passages, one feels the vibrancy of an ancient world in flux, wherein the message remains steadfast despite shifting contextual sands.

Exploring the Hebrew and Aramaic texts of the Bible reveals not just the technicalities of languages, but a gateway to understanding the spiritual odyssey of the people who spoke them. Each name, phrase, and even individual letter carries resonances of age-old traditions, offering modern readers a touchstone with the divine, beckoning them to deeper spiritual engagement. These languages, steeped in history and theology, weave narratives that traverse time and space, speaking to the core of human existence.

One cannot overlook the allure of Hebrew poetry, seen especially in books like Psalms and Song of Solomon, where the language is as much about sound as it is about meaning. The psalmist's cries reverberate—"The Lord is my shepherd; I shall not want" (Psalms. 23:1)—as does the echo of human longing and divine consolation through metaphoric imagery and parallelism, distinctive features of

Hebrew poetry. This linguistic artistry invites readers to not only understand but to feel the essence of worship and supplication.

As we turn to the Targums, Aramaic translations and interpretations of the Hebrew Bible, we find a critical bridge for understanding how ancient communities perceived the sacred text. These paraphrased interpretations provide a glimpse into theological and cultural shifts, allowing modern readers to fathom the manifold interpretations that Hebrew and Aramaic texts inspired even within their own times.

Aramaic also extends its reach into the New Testament. Most notably in the words of Christ on the cross, "Eli, Eli, lama sabachthani?" (Matthew 27:46). This cry, etched in Aramaic, encapsulates the human and the divine, illustrating the convergence of cultural and spiritual narratives. Such moments underscore how Aramaic threads through the Bible, piecing together the patchwork of human experience.

In discussing these original languages, we mustn't overlook the scribes and scholars through whom these texts have endured. Their meticulous preservation of language reflects a devotion to meaning that transcends mere words. The Hebrew and Aramaic scrolls have endured wars, migrations, and cultural revolutions, yet their essence remains unwavering and dynamic, a testament to the enduring nature of the sacred text itself.

Ultimately, studying the Hebrew and Aramaic texts of the Bible enables readers to imbibe the essence of a tradition that is both ancient and uniquely immediate. Each verse beckons with its symbolic depth and cultural richness, urging exploration beyond the surface. With each word, the languages ask not merely to be read, but to be experienced, allowing one's spirit to resonate with the echoes of prophets and kings, connecting across the ages. Through commitment to these original tongues, the Scriptures breathe anew, inspiring transformation and inviting readers to find their own stories within the divine narrative.

Greek Scriptures The journey into the heart of the Greek Scriptures opens a window into a world where the ancient and divine intersected with vibrant cultures of the Mediterranean. The New Testament, penned in Greek, holds a rich tapestry interwoven with historical narratives, poetic expressions, and philosophical thoughts. This language choice was not an accident; rather, it was an incredible providence that aligned with the Hellenistic era, a period where Greek culture and language dominated the Mediterranean basin. This strategic alignment ensured that the teachings of Jesus and the revelations given to early Christians reached a wide audience, transcending Jewish territories and infiltrating the corners of the known world.

The Greek language, known for its precision and expressive richness, was a vehicle capable of conveying theological concepts with remarkable clarity. Koine Greek, the dialect used in the New Testament, was the common language of the time, suitable for both scholarly discourse and everyday transactions. This accessibility was pivotal for spreading Christianity's message far beyond its Jewish roots. The New Testament texts, therefore, were not just sacred writings; they were also a tool of cultural bridge-building, drawing diverse audiences into a shared understanding of Christ's teachings.

Apart from linguistic prowess, Greek Scriptures encapsulate compelling narrative forms. Consider the Gospels, each depicting the life and ministry of Jesus Christ. They utilize parables, vivid stories with spiritual lessons, delivered in a manner that resonated deeply with those familiar with Greek rhetorical traditions. Jesus, through parables like the Good Samaritan (Luke 10:25-37) and the Prodigal Son (Luke 15:11-32), communicated profound moral truths in ways that invited reflection and introspection.

The Apostle Paul's epistles provide another dimension, showcasing how Greek allowed for complex theological arguments and philosophical discussions. Engaging with audiences that appreciated reason and debate, Paul's letters are replete with appeals to logic and moral reasoning. For instance, in Romans 12:2, Paul challenges believers to "be not conformed to this world: but be ye transformed by the renewing of your mind," urging a transformation that echoes both philosophical transformation known in Greek thought and spiritual rejuvenation (Romans 12:2).

While Koine Greek facilitated widespread communication, it also presented interpretive challenges. Each word reverberated with meanings layered over centuries and across cultural dimensions. Concepts like "agape" for love or "logos" for word carried philosophical weight and demanded careful consideration in translation and teaching. Misinterpretation could lead to significant theological divergence, making the study and understanding of these texts a pursuit requiring both scholarly rigor and divine guidance.

Greek Scriptures do more than convey the message of salvation; they are a testament to the early Church's struggle and resilience to define and defend its doctrines. The Book of Acts captures this beautifully, chronicling the Apostles' missionary journeys across regions dominated by Greek language and thought. The spread of the Gospel across cities like Corinth, Ephesus, and Athens showcases the dynamic interaction between emerging Christian beliefs and established Hellenistic philosophy. Paul engaging with Greek philosophers on Mars Hill (Acts 17:22-31) exemplifies this blend of intellectual discourse and spiritual revelation.

The preservation of Greek manuscripts over the centuries also reflects the devotion and precision of early Christian scholars. Texts like the Septuagint, the Greek translation of the Hebrew Scriptures, were integral in shaping early Christian theology and practice. The

Septuagint provided a scriptural foundation that the New Testament writers often quoted, bridging Old and New Covenant understandings and connecting communities across ethnic and cultural divides.

The Greek Scriptures' enduring legacy is not merely in their language but in their ability to translate divine mysteries into human understanding. By engaging with Greek thought, early Christians could articulate the mysteries of faith in terms that resonated with a broader audience seeking truth and meaning. This articulation was not just theological but transformative, encouraging believers to shape their lifestyles around the radical teachings of love, service, and sacrifice embodied by Christ.

Indeed, the Greek Scriptures invite readers today, as they did centuries ago, to delve into a journey of faith that transcends mere belief. They call for an evolution of the soul, reflecting the heart of teachings that emphasize inner transformation echoed in passages like "For God so loved the world, that he gave his only begotten Son, that whosoever believeth in him should not perish, but have everlasting life" (John 3:16). Such words continue to inspire, comfort, and challenge believers toward deeper spiritual truths.

In studying the Greek Scriptures, one can find not only a historical document but an ongoing dialogue between the divine and human. This dialogue invites us to see beyond the text's surface, to explore the mysteries of faith, and to find a connection with the broader narrative of God's work throughout history. As students of these writings, the journey involves embracing change, welcoming diverse perspectives, and ultimately, cultivating a profound relationship with the sacred text that continues to speak to humanity in every age, providing light, direction, and hope.

Translation Challenges and Triumphs

As we journey into "The Language of the Scriptures", we encounter the intricate tapestry woven by translation—an endeavor rich with both challenges and triumphs. The Bible, originally penned in Hebrew, Aramaic, and Greek, poses a formidable task for translators striving to preserve its divine essence while making it accessible to a contemporary audience. Translating sacred texts is not just about linguistic conversion; it's about conveying the spiritual and cultural context embedded within the original words. This delicate balancing act has historically led to both profound insights and occasional controversies.

Biblical translation first faced major hurdles with the Septuagint, the Greek translation of the Hebrew Scriptures. This endeavor, which started in the 3rd century BCE, was transformative. For the first time, the scriptures were available to those who did not speak Hebrew. Yet, translation can be a double-edged sword, as nuances can be easily lost. For instance, Greek lacks certain Hebrew poetic structures, making it challenging to preserve the rhythm and parallelism that characterize so much of the Hebrew text.

Consider the word "chesed," often rendered as "lovingkindness" or "mercy" in English. This Hebrew term is rich, encompassing concepts of covenant loyalty, love, and grace. No single English word captures its full depth. When "chesed" appears in the original text, translators must grapple with conveying its profound significance without losing its multifaceted nature. This struggle exemplifies the inherent complexity of translating ancient texts into modern languages.

In the New Testament, the Greek language presented its own array of challenges. As the lingua franca of the Roman Empire, Greek allowed the message of Jesus Christ to spread far and wide. However, translating Greek texts for future generations introduced the issue of cultural shifts. Phrases that resonated deeply in a Greco-Roman context might not convey the same meaning to diverse societies around the world. How do we translate Jesus' declaration, "I am the way, the truth, and the life" (John 14:6), so it remains meaningful across time and cultural barriers?

Another significant milestone in biblical translation was the advent of the Latin Vulgate by Jerome in the late 4th century CE. Jerome's work further opened the scriptures to a wider audience, but his choices also raised debates. Certain terms he selected sparked theological discussions that influenced the church for centuries. For example, Jerome's translation of the Greek "metanoia" as "penitentia" has spurred extensive discourse about repentance and penance in Christian theology.

With the dawn of the Reformation came a renewed emphasis on translating the Bible into vernacular languages. Martin Luther's German translation in 1534 played a pivotal role not only in religious reformation but also in shaping the modern German language. Translation now wasn't just a scholarly endeavor; it became a catalyst for social transformation. Luther's Bible democratized access to Scripture, laying the groundwork for personal interpretation and individual faith journeys.

The King James Version, completed in 1611, stands as one of the most celebrated translations in history. Its majestic prose and poetic resonance have left an indelible mark on English literature and religious life. Yet, its translators faced formidable decisions. They had to navigate linguistic ambiguities and theological nuances, striving for a text that honored the original languages while speaking to the faithful in a manner both precise and beautiful. Their work underscored how translation triumphs when it bridges ancient wisdom with contemporary relevance, echoing eternally with the command, "Let there be light" (Gen. 1:3).

In modern times, translation challenges persist as scholars work toward versions that reflect new understandings of ancient cultures and discoveries, like the Dead Sea Scrolls. These new insights offer fresh perspectives but also complicate translation efforts. Navigating the tension between textual fidelity and modern readability requires translators to be both sensitive and innovative. How can they maintain the depth of the Apostle Paul's epistles while ensuring they resonate clearly in today's world?

Each translation is a snapshot of a particular moment in time, blending the current language, culture, and theological emphasis of its creators with the timeless truths of the Bible. Innovations in technology have further broadened the reach and diversity of translations, enabling adaptations for different dialects and digital platforms. In this, there's triumph as more people access the scriptures than ever before, each reader invited into an ancient, yet ever-present, dialogue.

The continued evolution of biblical translation reminds us of a profound truth: the Scriptures, while rooted in history, are meant to live vibrantly in every age, speaking to every soul. As Isaiah proclaims, "The grass withereth, the flower fadeth: but the word of our God shall stand forever" (Isaiah 40:8). Translation ensures that this enduring word remains alive, resonating with new generations and guiding them as they seek understanding and connection with the divine.

Chapter 3:
The Cultural World of Genesis

As we embark on this exploration of Genesis, it's vital to appreciate the vibrant cultural tapestry that underpins its narratives. Genesis, the first book of the Bible, provides more than a historical account; it's a rich cultural canvas interwoven with ancient Near Eastern traditions and customs. This foundational text reveals the social structures, beliefs, and everyday practices of the time, painting a vivid picture of a world where clan affiliations and patriarchal hierarchies shaped community life. The stories within, from Adam and Eve to Joseph's rise in Egypt, are not only transformative spiritual lessons but also reflections of real societal landscapes. In Genesis, the divine covenants made with figures like Abraham offer insights into the theological understandings influencing ancient life and morality. "Now the Lord had said unto Abram, Get thee out of thy country, and from thy kindred, and from thy father's house, unto a land that I will shew thee" (Genesis 12:1). Such passages illuminate the relationship between God and humanity, dominated by promises and pilgrimages, highlighting a life centered on faith and purpose. This chapter invites us to see Genesis not just as a chronological unfolding of human events, but as the profound intersection of human culture and divine narrative, where each character's journey is a brushstroke contributing to the timeless masterpiece, inspiring readers to seek the divine within their own cultural contexts.

Social Structures in Genesis

In the unfolding narrative of Genesis, social structures emerge as vital pillars of ancient life, illuminating the intricate tapestry of relationships that defined early biblical communities. Patriarchal figures like Abraham, Isaac, and Jacob stand not just as individuals but also as cornerstones of familial and tribal identity. Within these familial clusters, the significance of covenants and birthrights illustrates a cultural system deeply rooted in kinship and lineage. We witness a society where the roles of men and women, as well as the dynamics between siblings, shape the unfolding of divine promises and human actions. For instance, Joseph's saga of dreams and deliverance reveals how familial ties can lead to both conflict and salvation, demonstrating the potent influence of social constructs ("Genesis. 37:5" to "Genesis. 50:21"). Genesis offers a profound insight into how these early social frameworks were not merely background details, but instrumental in the orchestration of God's will, showcasing that within the domains of home and community, the seeds of faith were sown and hopes nurtured, laying the foundation for the Israelite identity.

Family and Clan Dynamics in Genesis reflect the intricate tapestry of human relationships that form the backbone of this foundational biblical book. As we delve into the world of Genesis, it's essential to appreciate how family structures were not just social entities but spiritual ecosystems, echoing divine purposes and human aspirations. In these narratives, families are more than mere biological units; they are expressions of faith, obedience, and sometimes divine intervention.

From the opening pages of Genesis, family holds a crucial role. The creation narrative itself presents the family as an ordained institution, revealing God's intention for human companionship and multiplication. Adam and Eve's story is not just about individual choices but also about the profound effects those choices have on familial relations and subsequently the whole of humanity. 'And God blessed them, and God said unto them, Be fruitful, and multiply, and replenish the earth, and subdue it' (Genesis. 1:28). This commandment underscores the heart of family life in Genesis: propagation and stewardship of creation, both physically and spiritually.

As we move forward, the dynamics of family take on varying dimensions. The stories of Abraham, Isaac, Jacob, and Joseph demonstrate how familial bonds can become both a source of strength and tension. Abraham's journey illustrates how faith can bring blessings across generations, a theme seen in God's covenant with him: 'And in thy seed shall all the nations of the earth be blessed' (Genesis. 22:18). This promise is not merely a personal boon but a family legacy, impacting descendants and shaping human history.

Family dynamics in Genesis also reveal the complexities of human emotion and interaction. Relationships are fraught with love, jealousy, rivalry, and reconciliation. Take Isaac and Ishmael or Jacob and Esau—their stories mirror the struggles and reconciliations which many families face. These tales remind us that familial discord is not new to history, yet they also show paths to healing and understanding, as seen in Jacob's eventual reunion with Esau. This reconciliation offers a vision of hope and renewal, illustrating the power of forgiveness and divine orchestration.

The concept of the clan extends the idea of family into a larger social structure. Clans in Genesis represent extended kinship networks that share common goals, resources, and beliefs. They were crucial in maintaining identity and continuity, especially in a nomadic or semi-nomadic lifestyle. For instance, Jacob's family, which evolves into the twelve tribes of Israel, demonstrates how these clan structures function as foundational blocks for societal organization and development.

Interestingly, clan ties were not confined to biological links; they extended through marriage and alliances, as seen in the numerous kinship interactions throughout Genesis. These relationships were pivotal for survival and prosperity in ancient societal structures. The alliances between clans, exemplified by Abraham's covenant with God and subsequent interactions with other peoples and tribes, lay a framework for understanding communal living and mutual welfare.

Moreover, the role of women and matriarchs in these clan dynamics cannot be overlooked. Women like Sarah, Rebekah, Leah, and Rachel held significant influence within their families, often steering the course of events through their actions and decisions. Their narratives highlight the interplay of divine promise and human initiative, emphasizing that the weaving of family and clan stories is not a simple narrative of patriarchal dominance but a complex symphony involving all members.

In these intimate and large-scale dynamics, we find echoes of spiritual truths. Genesis teaches us that family is not just by blood but by shared faith and purpose. It illustrates that amid human flaws, grace and redemption can manifest. These stories inspire us to reflect on our own family and community relationships. Can we find in them the promise of future blessing, the potential for reconciliation, or the call to stewardship over God's creation?

The family and clan dynamics in Genesis compel us to see beyond ancient cultural contexts to timeless truths about human connection. They encourage a deepened understanding of how personal faith and communal identity interplay in forming the people of God. Through the luminous tapestry of Genesis, we are invited to explore not just our ancestry, but our shared destiny, as we navigate our faith journeys within the families and communities we inhabit today.

Theological Themes in Genesis

The Book of Genesis, with its rich tapestry of narratives, is not just an ancient chronicle but a profound exposition of foundational theological themes. As we delve into its depths, we discover timeless truths that are as relevant today as they were in the beginnings of biblical history. In essence, Genesis is not only about the creation of the world but about the creation of relationships—between God and humanity, among humans themselves, and with the world at large.

The first chapter of Genesis introduces us to the majestic account of creation, establishing the doctrine of God's sovereignty over the universe. "In the beginning God created the heaven and the earth" (Genesis 1:1). This declaration sets the stage for the entire biblical narrative, affirming that all of creation is an intentional act by a divine Creator. This foundational truth underscores God's omnipotence and wisdom, laying the groundwork for understanding the world as a place governed by His purposes and design.

Creation is not merely about divine power; it introduces God's inherent goodness. We repeatedly see God viewing creation as "good" and culminating in the creation of humanity as "very good" (Genesis 1:31). This emphasis on goodness highlights the perfection of God's work and His desire for harmony within His creation. It speaks to the intrinsic value of the world and humanity, which can inspire a sense of responsibility for maintaining the sanctity of life and the environment.

Another profound theme established in Genesis is the imago Dei, or the image of God, as it relates to humanity. "So God created man in his own image, in the image of God created he him; male and female created he them" (Genesis 1:27). This concept bestows a unique dignity and purpose upon every human being. It conveys an implied invitation to humans to reflect God's character through stewardship, creativity, and relationships.

The narrative shifts dramatically with the account of the Fall in Genesis 3, introducing the theme of sin and separation. When Adam and Eve disobey God's command, it results in a rupture in the divine-human relationship. This event is pivotal as it leads to an understanding of humanity's propensity for sin and the subsequent need for redemption. The verse "And the eyes of them both were opened, and they knew that they were naked" (Genesis 3:7) symbolizes a loss of innocence and the beginning of human self-awareness of sin.

Yet, even in judgment, there is the promise of restoration and hope. Genesis hints at God's plan for redemption with the protoevangelium, the first gospel, where God promises that the seed of the woman will crush the serpent's head (Genesis 3:15). This verse implies the future coming of a savior, woven into the fabric of Genesis as a beacon of hope amidst the darkness of the fall.

Genesis further explores the theme of God's covenantal relationships with humanity. The covenants with Noah, Abraham, Isaac, and Jacob illustrate God's unyielding faithfulness and commitment to His creation despite human failure. The Abrahamic covenant, where God promises to make Abraham "a great nation" and that "in thee shall all families of the earth be blessed" (Genesis 12:2-3), is particularly significant. It introduces the idea of a chosen people through whom God plans to usher in blessing and redemption for all nations.

Moreover, Genesis explores themes of faith and obedience through its patriarchs. The trials and triumphs of figures like Abraham, who "believed in the Lord; and he counted it to him for righteousness" (Genesis 15:6), serve as didactic models. These narratives invite readers to understand faith as an active trust in God's promises, even when circumstances seem daunting.

The interplay of divine justice and mercy is another crucial theme. We see God's justice manifest in the judgment of nations and individuals, like Sodom and Gomorrah, yet His mercy shines through in His willingness to spare the righteous (Genesis 18:23-32). This balance between justice and mercy provides a nuanced picture of God's character, guiding the reader to grasp the complexity of His dealings with humanity.

Genesis also reveals the power of God's presence and guidance. Through theophanies and divine encounters, characters like Jacob are transformed. Jacob's dream of a ladder reaching to heaven, where God reiterates His covenant, symbolizes the connection between the divine and the human realms (Genesis 28:12-15). Such narratives instill a sense of assurance that God is actively involved in the affairs of humankind.

Genealogies scattered throughout Genesis emphasize continuity and the unfolding of God's plan through generations. Each name holds a place in God's redemptive history, underscoring the theme of providence. Even when human plans falter, like Joseph's brothers selling him into slavery, God's purpose prevails, highlighted in Joseph's proclamation: "But as for you, ye thought evil against me; but God meant it unto good" (Genesis 50:20).

In conclusion, Genesis, with its profound theological themes, offers rich insights into humanity's relationship with God and the created world. It invites us to reflect on the paradigms of faith, the reality of sin, and the promise of salvation. As we journey through its narratives, Genesis compels us to see God's hand in history and our lives, encouraging an exploration of these truths through personal and communal lenses, guiding us toward a greater understanding of our place within God's grand design.

Chapter 4:
Exodus and the Birth of a Nation

The unfolding drama of Exodus marks the profound transition from slavery to liberation, chronicling not just a movement of people, but the emergence of a national identity bound by a covenant with the divine. This chapter highlights the pivotal moment when the Israelites, once shackled in Egyptian bondage, heed the call of Moses, a prophet chosen by God, to step into their destinies as a nation set apart. Guided by a pillar of cloud by day and fire by night, their journey through the wilderness represents both a physical and spiritual transformation. Here, the merging of cultural elements—such as the influence of Egyptian customs with newfound spiritual revelations—births a unique identity that stands resilient against time. As they wander, the establishment of laws and practices given at Mount Sinai forms a distinctive societal structure, rooted deeply in the promise and presence of Yahweh. "And I will take you to me for a people, and I will be to you a God" (Exodus 6:7) encapsulates the burgeoning relationship and solemn commitment between God and Israel. This momentous exodus transcends a historical event, serving as an enduring symbol of hope, faith, and the relentless pursuit of freedom against all odds.

Cultural Influences in Exodus

The book of Exodus isn't just a historical narrative; it's a vivid tapestry woven with cultural threads, largely influenced by the Egyptian civilization that shaped the Israelites' early experiences. Living in Egypt for centuries, the Israelites were in constant interaction with Egyptian customs and traditions, which impacted their social practices, language, and spiritual understanding. For example, the concept of sacred rituals and priestly orders reflects the structured religious milieu of Egypt. These influences can be discerned in the early legal frameworks and societal rules that Moses introduced to the fledgling nation, drawing parallels with Egyptian law. Even the architectural designs and motifs pervasive in early Israelite society echo Egyptian artistry. As the Israelites navigated their burgeoning identity, the Exodus journey became a profound crucible, blending their inherited Egyptian background with their divine calling. This fusion is pivotal as it portrays how cultural integration and divine revelation can coexist and shape a nation reliant on faith and obedience: "And Moses stretched forth his hand over the sea; and the Lord caused the sea to go back by a strong east wind all that night" (Exodus 14:21). Here, the cultural backdrop of a world influenced by mighty empires meets the transformative power of divine intervention, inspiring believers to recognize that cultural contexts can deepen their understanding of Scripture's eternal truths.

Egyptian Customs and Traditions interweave through the narrative of Exodus, offering us profound insight into the cultural milieu from which the Israelite nation emerged. The Egyptians, known for their rich and intricate society, significantly influenced the lives of the Hebrews, who resided amongst them for over four centuries. This profound integration and eventual differentiation from Egyptian customs provided the backdrop against which God's mighty act of deliverance unfolded, as recounted in the biblical narrative (Exodus 1:8-14).

In ancient Egypt, religion was woven into the very fabric of daily life, dominating from the towering temples of Thebes to the modest homes along the Nile. The pantheon of gods, led by figures such as Ra, the sun god, and Osiris, the god of the afterlife, played pivotal roles in shaping the spiritual and cultural ethos of the time. This polytheistic worldview starkly contrasted with the emerging monotheism of the Israelites, who worshipped Yahweh. The Egyptians' spiritual practices and ceremonial rites, most notably the elaborate funerary customs, underscored their belief in an afterlife and the cyclical nature of life and death. Such practices included mummification and the construction of monumental pyramids, which served as eternal resting places for their kings, or Pharaohs, believed to be divine beings themselves.

The Pharaohs, seen as both god and king, ruled with absolute authority, embodying the convergence of divine right and political power. This form of governance was pivotal in maintaining Egypt's societal structure, wherein a vast administrative bureaucracy underpinned a stratified society. At the apex stood the Pharaoh, followed by nobles, priests, scribes, craftsmen, and farmers, with slaves occupying the lowest rung. This rigid hierarchy was reflected in every aspect of life, from the grand palaces to the tasks performed by the Hebrews, who toiled in brick-making and construction (Exodus 5:6-19).

Considering the daily life of an Egyptian, we observe a civilization deeply rooted in agrarian practices, intimately connected with the Nile's rhythms. The annual flooding of the Nile provided fertile soil, ensuring abundant harvests, which were critical not just for sustenance but as a means of social stability and economic power. This connection to the land and reliance on predictable natural phenomena shaped Egyptian cultural attitudes towards order, predictability, and control over chaos—concepts intertwined with the divine order, or Ma'at, which governed their worldview. Ma'at, often personified as a goddess, represented truth, harmony, and justice, elements enshrined in both law and myth.

The diet of the ancient Egyptians also reveals much about their customs and social life. Common meals included bread and beer, staples consuming a significant part of the diet, supplemented by vegetables, fruit, and occasional meat or fish. This diet symbolizes sustenance and stability provided by the fertile banks of the Nile, also serving to distinguish classes, as nobility had access to more diverse food sources and lavish banquets.

Art and architecture stand as testaments to the Egyptians' enduring legacy. The grandeur of structures such as temples and tombs, adorned with intricate hieroglyphics and vibrant murals, narrate tales of gods and triumphs, asserting power and faith. These artistic expressions carried a deep symbolic meaning, reflecting their understanding of the divine and human worlds. Moreover, they encapsulate the Egyptians' penchant for order, symmetry, and permanence, contrasting sharply with the nomadic, transient existence of the Israelites during and after the Exodus.

The fusion of the Israelites and Egyptian customs went beyond economy, societal roles, and religion; it extended into language and cultural expressions. The Hebrews, immersed in Egyptian culture, inevitably absorbed linguistic elements, as seen in proper names and certain terms within the biblical text, indicative of this interchange. Moreover, the Egyptians' usage of a solar calendar and timekeeping systems likely influenced the Hebrews' structuring of their own time-related rituals and observances, hinting at cultural syncretism even within religious practices.

The influence of Egyptian customs is equally evident in the narrative motifs and theological themes within Exodus. The confrontation between Moses and Pharaoh is not merely a political struggle but a divine contest. The plagues, which assault Egypt's natural and spiritual order, challenge the very fabric of Egyptian belief and social structure, climaxing in the dramatic crossing of the Red Sea

(Exodus 14:21-31). This act, symbolizing chaos conquering order through divine intervention, reverses the Egyptian emphasis on stability and control, heralding the emergence of a new nation devoted to Yahweh.

Furthermore, the complex relationship between Egyptian magic and Hebrew miracles presents another layer of cultural interaction. The magicians in Pharaoh's court, versed in spells and enchantments, serve to juxtapose the power of God with human artifice (Exodus 7:11-12). This interplay underscores a compelling narrative of faith and divine supremacy, echoing through centuries of biblical interpretation.

The lasting impact of Egyptian customs and traditions helped shape the Israelites' collective memory as they transitioned from slaves to a sovereign people. Elsewhere in Scripture, such as in the Psalms and Prophets, reflections and echoes of this cultural exchange resurface, serving as reminders of God's deliverance and the transformation from bondage into a distinct identity founded upon faith and covenant.

Thus, understanding Egyptian customs isn't merely an academic exercise; it enriches our grasp of the biblical narrative, underscoring the plentiful tapestry from which the Jewish faith emerged. We are reminded of a God who works through history and culture, transforming ordinary human experiences into epic stories of faith, liberation, and identity. It invites us to look beyond the pages to the principles that govern divine interaction with humanity, encouraging personal reflection on the broader journey from captivity to freedom, in whatever form that may take in our own lives.

Theological Implications of the Exodus

The Exodus narrative isn't just a captivating story of liberation; it holds profound theological significance that resonates across ages. As the Israelites transitioned from enslavement in Egypt to freedom, they embarked on a journey of becoming God's chosen people, a nation uniquely set apart with a divine purpose. This transformation from a group of enslaved individuals to a covenant community is essential in understanding the theological fabric of the Bible.

At the heart of the Exodus is the divine revelation of God's character—His power, faithfulness, and justice. Through miraculous acts, such as the plagues that befell Egypt and the parting of the Red Sea, God demonstrated His supremacy over the deities of Egypt, affirming the Hebrews' belief in the one true God. "For I will pass through the land of Egypt this night, and will smite all the firstborn in the land of Egypt, both man and beast; and against all the gods of Egypt I will execute judgment: I am the Lord" (Exodus 12:12). These divine judgments were not only acts of liberation but declarations of theological truths: that God is both judge and deliverer.

This portrayal of God as Redeemer, emphasized through the Passover event, becomes a cornerstone of Israelite identity. The commandment to celebrate the Passover annually ensures that future generations never forget God's saving power and the deliverance from bondage. It's in these rituals and remembrances that theological themes of covenant and memory intertwine, creating a rhythm of remembrance that echoes throughout the Scriptures. This ritual has left an indelible mark not just on Jewish theology, but it also flows into Christian thought as a prefiguration of redemption through Christ.

Covenant theology is another critical implication that emerges from the Exodus narrative. God establishes a covenant with the people of Israel at Mount Sinai, providing them with the Law through which they would understand and enact their relationship with Him. The Ten Commandments, referred to biblically as "the words of the covenant, the ten commandments" (Exodus 34:28), symbolize the core principles upon which this new society was to be built. These aren't merely legal stipulations but foundational moral principles that reflect God's holiness and justice.

The faith journey of Israel, marked by their trials and triumphs in the wilderness, uncovers God's patience and mercy, illustrating that divine relationships are complex and multifaceted. Despite their frequent disobedience and complaints, evidenced by their longing to return to Egypt when faced with hardships, God's grace persists. This grace, however, isn't without expectations of transformation and fidelity from the Israelites. The theological tensions between divine sovereignty and human responsibility thus play out vibrantly within these passages, allowing for a nuanced exploration of what it means to walk in faith.

Moreover, the Exodus signifies the origination of a narrative framework that offers hope, justice, and salvation—a motif repeated through the Bible. The New Testament writers often draw on the imagery and themes of the Exodus to explain and underscore the work of Christ. The concept of Jesus as the Paschal Lamb in the Christian tradition is intrinsically linked to the Passover lamb of Exodus, highlighting a continuity in God's salvific history that spans both Testaments.

Furthermore, the theological implications extend beyond Israel and into universal questions of liberation and justice. The Exodus narrative has inspired numerous movements and figures throughout history, including the African American civil rights movement, to see their struggles for freedom through the lens of Exodus. Such an interpretation relies on the profound understanding that God's deliverance is not limited by time or space but is a persistent promise of justice against oppression.

The theological journey through Exodus also accentuates the vital role of leadership and faithfulness. Figures like Moses highlight God's use of human agency to fulfill divine purposes. Moses' transformation from a reluctant spokesperson to a paramount prophet teaches us that leadership in the eyes of God isn't about ability but availability and obedience. The interactions between God and Moses reveal relational aspects of divine communication, illustrating prayer and intercession as central to communal and national identity.

The language of covenant assurance and divine promises reverberates throughout the prophetic literature and even into the New Testament, resonating with ideas of restoration and eschatological hope. The ultimate fulfillment of God's promises becomes theologically entwined with both past deliverance and future redemption, reinforcing a cyclical pattern of hope and renewal evident in biblical narrative theology.

In contemporary discussions, the theological implications of the Exodus continue to challenge and inspire. They call for introspection on justice, leadership, and community while encouraging an exploration of God's character that is both intimate and transcendent. The Exodus teaches that liberation is inextricably linked to moral responsibility and communal expression of faith.

As we draw connections from this ancient story to modern contexts, these theological themes remain vibrant. The faith journey, marked by trial and divine intervention, echoes the perennial human longing for freedom, justice, and a deeper connection with the divine. The Exodus, with its rich tapestry of liberation and covenant, invites believers and seekers alike to ponder their place within God's continuing story of redemption.

Ultimately, the theological implications of the Exodus serve as a reminder of the enduring power of faith and the transformational possibilities inherent in divine promise. It calls us to trust in a God who sees, hears, and acts—a God who liberates us not just from physical bondage, but also from the limitations of fear and doubt, encouraging us toward a journey into His promised freedom.

Chapter 5: Kings and Prophets

As we delve into the era of Kings and Prophets, we witness a fascinating tapestry of history and divine interaction where the sovereignty of God interweaves with human governance. This period, marked by the rise and fall of Israel's monarchies, reveals a profound narrative of leadership, obedience, and often, rebellion. The kings of Israel, entrusted with steering a theocratic nation, faced challenges that tested their allegiance to God amidst a backdrop of political intrigue and external threats. Meanwhile, prophets emerged as divine messengers, wielding the dual power of vision and voice to guide, rebuke, and inspire a nation often torn between covenant fidelity and worldly allure. Figures like Samuel, Elijah, and Isaiah stand as stalwart witnesses to God's relentless pursuit of His people, reminding us that divine guidance was never far, even when the throne's occupants faltered. These prophets called the nation back to its spiritual roots, emphasizing righteousness and justice in accordance with the words of the Lord: "For I desired mercy, and not sacrifice; and the knowledge of God more than burnt offerings" (Hosea 6:6). Their proclamations pushed against the boundaries of mere human governance, urging both king and country to align with the divine will and revealing the enduring truth that God's kingdom transcends earthly thrones.

The Monarchical Period

The Monarchical Period marks a pivotal chapter in Israel's history, filled with tales of might, divine mandates, and human ambition. This era unveils the transformation from a fragmented collection of tribes to a centralized nation under unified leadership, guided by kings who were seen not just as rulers, but as divinely appointed stewards. Through the coronations and reigns of Saul, David, and Solomon, we witness the tension between earthly power and divine counsel, capturing the essence of God's covenant with His people. David's passion for God, despite his fallibility, is a profound reminder of grace, where "the Lord looketh on the heart" (1 Samuel 16:7). Solomon's wisdom invites us to delve into the pursuit of understanding, yet his monarchy warns of the perils of pride and idolatry, urging us to align with divine wisdom. These narratives offer more than historical accounts; they are timeless lessons on leadership, faith, and the unwavering promise of God's presence, urging believers to find strength in their appointed truths.

Kingship and Governance in Israel captures a significant era in Israel's history that saw the rise of monarchs who were as much political figures as they were spiritual and military leaders. This period, known as the Monarchical Period, marks a transformative era in the theocratic governance of Israel, highlighted by the intersection of divine guidance and earthly rule. It invites us to consider how leadership and spirituality were woven together in the tapestry of Israelite society.

The inception of kingship in Israel came as the people clamored for a human leader to guide them through the political complexities that surrounded them. They yearned for someone to unify the tribes and present a formidable front against their enemies. Despite God's initial reluctance, the Israelites' insistent plea for a king like the neighboring nations saw the eventual rise of Saul as the first monarch (1 Samuel 8:5). This transition from a tribal confederacy to a centralized monarchy was pivotal in altering the cultural and administrative landscape of Israel.

In these early years under Saul, Israel navigated the challenges of kingship. Saul's reign was marked by an enthusiastic start, but it eventually faced turbulence due to his failure to fully adhere to divine commandments, illustrating the peril of leaders veering from God's path. Saul's inability to obey God's instructions led to his downfall, serving as a cautionary tale of governance gone astray.

The subsequent reign of David, anointed by Samuel as Saul's successor, brought about a flourishing of Israelite monarchy. David's leadership was transformational, not only because of his military conquests which expanded Israel's borders but also due to his spiritual devotion and belief in God's sovereignty. "The Lord is my shepherd; I shall not want" (Psalms 23:1), David declares, illustrating a profound reliance on God's guidance that underpinned his governance. Under David, Jerusalem was established as the political and spiritual center, a unifying move that symbolized the consolidation of the tribes into a cohesive entity.

With David's son Solomon, the Israelite kingdom reached its zenith in terms of wealth, cultural achievements, and international influence. Solomon's reign was renowned for wisdom and prosperity, underpinning Israel's golden age. His construction of the temple in Jerusalem provided a permanent dwelling for the Ark of the Covenant, symbolizing God's everlasting covenant with Israel and serving as a central place of worship. Proverbs sprang from the wisdom for which Solomon was famous, teaching lessons on governance, justice, and divine favor.

Yet, even with Solomon's illustrious reign, there were cracks beneath the surface. His extravagant building projects and lavish lifestyle strained the kingdom's resources, while alliances made through numerous marriages introduced foreign influences that clashed with Israel's spiritual foundations. As Solomon turned to other deities, forsaking God's commandments, we see the inevitable decline that often shadows unchecked power.

Following Solomon's rule, the kingdom fractured into the northern kingdom of Israel and the southern kingdom of Judah, a division that notably changed the political and spiritual dynamics of the region. This split highlighted the vulnerability and limitations of human governance that lacks consistent divine allegiance. Each kingdom had its own struggles with idolatry and political instability, punctuated by the presence of prophets who served as God's mouthpieces in calling both people and kings back to righteousness.

Throughout these narratives, prophets like Elijah, Elisha, Isaiah, and Jeremiah stood as pivotal figures. They provided counsel, warned of impending consequences for disobedience, and offered hope for restoration. These prophets are best understood not as mere bearers of doom, but as voices of conscience and hope, highlighting the inseparable nature of righteous governance and steadfast faith in Yahweh.

The Kingship and Governance in Israel era showcases what it means for leaders to wield authority while being accountable to divine expectations. Kings were not autonomous nor absolute in their power; they, too, were called to humility and the guiding principles of Mosaic Law. "He that ruleth over men must be just, ruling in the fear of God" (2 Samuel 23:3). This balance of power and piety is a timeless lesson on leadership under divine mandate.

As one reflects on this period, recognizing its failures and successes, it prompts today's leaders and believers alike to heed the intertwined demands of justice, mercy, and a steadfast heart obedient to God. The monarchy, while a distinct cultural and historical construct, offers rich insights into the perennial dance between temporal authority and divine guidance.

In summation, the Monarchical Period in Israel's history presents profound teachings on leadership, faith, and the social constructs that govern human relations. By understanding the cultural and divine forces at play, modern readers can gain insights into the nuances of effective governance—insights characterized by humility before God, wise judgment, and the unwavering pursuit of peace and righteousness.

The Role of Prophets in Israelite Culture

In the vibrant tapestry of Israelite culture, few figures stand as prominently as the prophets. These individuals, chosen by God, played pivotal roles that transcended mere spiritual guidance; they were the bridges between the divine and the earthly realm. Unlike kings, whose authority stemmed from earthly power and governance, prophets drew their influence from a higher source. This bestowed upon them a unique combination of reverence and responsibility, setting them apart as vital instruments of God's will.

The role of prophets was multifaceted, encompassing not just religious instructions but also social and political commentary. In a time when moral, ethical, and societal structures often teetered on fragile foundations, the prophets were called upon to deliver unvarnished truths. This duty was both a privilege and a burden, as the divine messages they carried frequently challenged the status quo. They called upon the people of Israel to remember the covenant and adhere to God's laws, often reminding them of the consequences if they failed to do so, as reflected in Amos 3:7, "Surely the Lord God will do nothing, but he revealeth his secret unto his servants the prophets."

In a society predominantly led by kings, prophets served as a divine check on secular power. While kings were charged with ruling the nation, it was the prophets who provided spiritual and ethical guidance. This dynamic often led to tension as prophets confronted kings over ethical missteps or spiritual neglect. In the case of Nathan's confrontation with King David after the incident with Bathsheba, for instance, the prophet's courage and clarity were evident. Nathan did not shy away from delivering God's rebuke, highlighting the prophet's critical role as a moral compass (2 Samuel 12:7).

The prophetic office was not hereditary; it was a calling that transcended familial lines. God chose those He deemed fit, often from unexpected backgrounds. Amos, for instance, was a humble shepherd and fig farmer before he was called to prophesy to Israel (Amos 7:14-15). This diversity underscored the principle that God values sincere devotion and willingness to serve over worldly status or lineage. It speaks to the heart of Israelite values where devotion to God and justice outweighed societal hierarchy and birthright.

In addition to their roles as spiritual advisers and political critics, prophets also served as harbingers of hope. They spoke promises of restoration in times of despair and trials. When the Israelites faced exile or conquest, prophetic voices like Jeremiah and Isaiah assured them of God's enduring covenant and eventual deliverance. Such messages provided hope and resilience to a beleaguered people, affirming that even in dire circumstances, God had not forsaken them. As Isaiah boldly declared, "For I am with thee to save thee and to deliver thee, saith the Lord" (Isaiah 43:10).

Furthermore, prophets acted as cultural historians and theologians. Through narratives, poetry, and symbolic acts, they recorded and preserved the spiritual heritage of Israel for future generations. Their writings formed a significant portion of what is now the Hebrew Bible, offering insights into Israel's theological evolution and its understanding of God through successive epochs. Prophetical books became treasure troves of wisdom, rich in cultural, ethical, and spiritual significance.

While prophets were often revered, they were not without opposition. Their messages were at times unpopular, especially when addressing sin and demanding repentance. Nevertheless, their commitment to truth, even in the face of persecution, served as a testament to their dedication to God's mission. Elijah's confrontation with the prophets of Baal (1 Kings 18:20-40) and Jeremiah's unyielding call for repentance amidst threats are but a few examples of the intense challenges prophets faced.

It's also crucial to consider the communal role played by prophets. They often gathered schools of disciples, perpetuating their teachings and establishing prophetic communities. Such groups were essential in sustaining and disseminating the prophetic tradition, ensuring that the prophetic voice continued to resonate within Israelite society even after the demise of individual prophets.

The intricate dance between prophets and culture in ancient Israel highlights a profound lesson for believers today: the divine mandate for justice, righteousness, and adherence to God's vision remains as relevant now as it was then. Prophets called people to live authentically and aligned with divine principles, a calling that transcends the ages and beckons each generation anew. It is a reminder that while human leaders may falter, the divine truth through prophetic voices remains ever constant, a beacon lighting the path in times of moral ambiguity.

In reflecting on the role of prophets, we uncover a mosaic of courage, faith, and divine purpose that speaks volumes about the unending relationship between humanity and the divine. Prophets are not just figures of the past; they symbolize the timeless quest for truth and an unwavering commitment to God's will. As we delve into their stories, we are encouraged to listen, learn, and perhaps find our voice in the ongoing narrative of faith.

Chapter 6: Wisdom Literature

Delving into the profound realm of Wisdom Literature, we encounter a tapestry of reflection and insight woven into the fabric of biblical texts like Proverbs and Ecclesiastes. These books are more than mere collections of wise sayings; they offer a window into the values, ethics, and daily life of ancient Israel. Proverbs, with its pithy observations, embodies the essence of practical wisdom, delivering lessons on morality and prudent living that resonate across cultures and epochs. It paints vivid scenes of agrarian life, familial relationships, and the divine ordering of the cosmos, reminding us that "Happy is the man that findeth wisdom" (Proverbs 3:13). Meanwhile, Ecclesiastes ventures into the philosophical, probing the depths of human existence and the pursuit of meaning amidst the transience of life. Its timeless inquiry—"What profit hath a man of all his labor which he taketh under the sun?" (Ecclesiastes 1:3)—beckons readers to explore what lies beyond the pursuit of temporal gains. Both texts, distinct yet complementary, invite us into a dance between the divine wisdom imparted by God and the human quest for understanding, a compelling reminder of the enduring relationship between faith and reason.

Cultural Insights from Proverbs

In the dynamic tapestry of biblical wisdom literature, Proverbs stands as a luminous guide, offering profound insights into the cultural fabric of ancient Israel. Its verses, woven with vivid imagery and practical teachings, reflect the everyday life and social norms of a people deeply rooted in community values and spiritual wisdom. Proverbs encapsulates the essence of timeless wisdom that addresses universal themes, such as the value of hard work, the importance of integrity, and the impact of words, which resonate with the rhythms of daily existence. These ancient sayings also illustrate a society where the oral tradition was vital, and each proverb served not just as instruction but as a cornerstone of cultural identity. Through Proverbs, we glimpse a culture where wisdom was esteemed and passed down through generations to guide moral and ethical living. As Solomon declared, "A wise man will hear, and will increase learning; and a man of understanding shall attain unto wise counsels" (Proverbs 1:5), emphasizing a pursuit of knowledge that transcends time while anchoring us in the cultural heritage that shaped these enduring truths.

Daily Life Reflected in Proverbs serves as a fascinating glimpse into the ancient world, offering pearls of wisdom that resonate through time. In these succinct nuggets of insight, we find echoes of the day-to-day lives of those who lived in biblical times, offering a rare window into their world and a mirror to ours. The simple yet profound teachings of Proverbs encapsulate lessons from ordinary experiences, reminding us of the timelessness of human nature and the enduring values that bind us across generations.

Proverbs, with their brevity and punch, reflect truths steeped in the rhythm of daily life—its joys and struggles, its challenges and triumphs. As we dissect these ancient sayings, we observe that their inspiration is drawn not from grand historical events but from mundane, everyday affairs. It's the farmer, the merchant, and the craftsman who leap off the pages, infusing each proverb with the authenticity of lived experience. The biblical proverb, "A soft answer turneth away wrath: but grievous words stir up anger" (Proverbs 15:1), vividly captures this ethos, speaking directly to interpersonal relationships and the power of communication in daily interactions.

Everyday life in ancient Israel—its values, principles, and societal norms—gives life to these proverbs. They teach us about the collective wisdom that ordinary people accumulated over time by observing the world around them. For instance, the agricultural metaphors frequently used in Proverbs reflect a community living close to the land. Regular encounters with the cycles of sowing and harvest, the reliance on rain, and the aphorisms about diligence are clear reminders that farming was central to their existence. "He that tilleth his land shall be satisfied with bread: but he that followeth vain persons is void of understanding" (Proverbs 12:11) speaks to the value of hard work and its direct correlation to sustenance, a connotation that still resonates deeply today.

Furthermore, Proverbs articulate social observations that were not only relevant to their times but also carry an enduring significance for us. Idleness and work ethic are recurring themes. The cautionary tale of the sluggard—"Go to the ant, thou sluggard; consider her ways, and be wise" (Proverbs 6:6)—serves as a beacon for industriousness, underscoring the necessity of planning and active engagement in work to ensure prosperity. These teachings transcend their era, challenging us to reflect on our work ethic in a world that often encourages shortcuts to success.

The family unit, a cornerstone of societal structure, emerges vividly through Proverbs. Instructions regarding familial relationships emphasize values that were paramount in ancient societies. "Train up a child in the way he should go: and when he is old, he will not depart from it" (Proverbs 22:6) captures a universal truth about parenting—the importance of establishing a strong foundation for the future. These insights into familial bonds reveal how deeply entrenched the values of discipline, education, and moral guidance were within the ancient community.

Proverbs not only address personal and family matters but extend their reach to community and societal dynamics as well. Respectful and honest interactions with others are a frequent theme, underscoring the importance of integrity. "Wealth gotten by vanity shall be diminished: but he that gathereth by labour shall increase" (Proverbs 13:11) speaks to the ethical standards regarding wealth accumulation, advocating for honesty over deceit in financial dealings. The community, thus, relied on the ethical underpinning of each individual to function harmoniously.

Adding to this tapestry of daily wisdom is the nuanced understanding of human emotions and reactions. The urge to respect emotions while maintaining control over them is captured in proverbial wisdom, which offers guidance on navigating the labyrinth of human feelings. For instance, the injunction to control anger or to understand the pitfalls of pride highlights the biblical insights into human psychology long before it became a formalized field of study. Embracing humility and extending patience are virtues praised, illuminating a path toward inner peace and societal harmony that still holds relevance in modern times.

The ritual and spiritual life interwoven into their daily expressions reveal a reverence for divine guidance that permeated every aspect of existence. Proverbs like "The fear of the Lord is the beginning of knowledge: but fools despise wisdom and instruction" (Proverbs 1:7) show a society deeply rooted in spiritual and ethical contemplations, recognizing divine wisdom as the ultimate source of all understanding. This spiritual context provided a framework within which daily life was lived, offering instructions for both moral and practical living.

At their core, Proverbs seek to foster a deep respect for learning and wisdom. The constant exhortations to pursue wisdom reflect an aspiration towards betterment that was as pertinent then as it is now. In a world characterized by rapid change, the ancient call to wisdom compels us to pause, reflect, and seek the timeless truths that offer clarity in our modern context.

While rooted in a specific cultural milieu, the wisdom encapsulated in Proverbs transcends its immediate context to offer guidance on universal human issues. Its teachings foster resilience and adaptability, essential qualities for navigating the complexities of contemporary life. The proverbs encourage a reflective mindset, urging individuals to glean insight from observations and experiences, thereby enriching their journey through life.

In a world increasingly driven by technology and digital experiences, the ancient wisdom of Proverbs whispers timeless truths that call us back to the essential elements of human existence. It bridges the ancient and the modern, offering us the depth of insight gleaned from centuries of lived experience. As we engage with these teachings, we find not only a reflection of ancient daily life but also a mirror through which we can examine our paths and choices.

This section of our exploration into Wisdom Literature challenges us to delve deeply into Proverbs, to extract lessons that apply to our lives with renewed vigor and insight. The proverbs reveal that the fundamental aspects of our humanity—the need for connection, purpose, and understanding—remain unchanged. In embracing the wisdom of yesterday, we empower ourselves to build a meaningful tomorrow.

Ecclesiastes and the Search for Meaning

In the midst of the vast tapestry that is the wisdom literature of the Bible lies the enigmatic book of Ecclesiastes, a text whose very essence questions the nature of existence, confronting the perplexities of life's inherent meaning. Ecclesiastes, traditionally attributed to King

Solomon, invites readers to reflect deeply on the transient and often elusive pursuit of fulfillment in our day-to-day lives. Where other wisdom books such as Proverbs offer clear-cut insights and instructions, Ecclesiastes delves into the complexities of human experience with a tone that is both contemplative and provocatively honest.

"Vanity of vanities, saith the Preacher, vanity of vanities; all is vanity" (Ecclesiastes 1:2). This opening declaration sets the tone for a journey that explores the limitations of human wisdom and the ephemeral nature of worldly pursuits. The term "vanity" here isn't about self-absorption but rather derived from the Hebrew "hevel," meaning vapors or breaths, suggesting impermanence. Through this lens, the author, referred to as the Preacher or Qohelet, examines the futility of striving for wealth, wisdom, and pleasure as finite goals.

The cultural backdrop of Ecclesiastes is vital to understanding its reflections. In the ancient Near Eastern context, where stability was scarce and life often unpredictable, the pursuit of security through material and intellectual achievements was as alluring then as it is today. However, Ecclesiastes provides a counter-narrative, challenging its audience to re-evaluate what constitutes a meaningful life. Through its poetic ruminations, the text questions societal norms, urging an introspective journey rather than mere conformance to established paths.

Amid the seeming melancholy of its reflections, Ecclesiastes doesn't leave its readers without hope. Subtly woven through its discourse is an underlying message: the recognition of life's transience can lead to a greater appreciation of the divine, inviting believers to trust in God's eternal plan. This book encourages an existential humility, a reminder that human understanding is limited, and that ultimate knowledge lies with God. It nudges us to embrace the uncertainty of life with a faith that transcends the material world.

The juxtaposition of life's fleeting pleasures against the eternal wisdom of God is a theme that resonates with modern readers just as it did with ancient audiences. In a world that often equates success with the accumulation of wealth and status, Ecclesiastes provides a prophetic voice, reminding us that joy and contentment are found in the simplicity of living in alignment with divine purpose. Through this reflection, readers discover that meaning is not derived from external achievements but from an inner alignment with divine principles.

The tension between despair and hope, between the earthly and the eternal, is a profound dance that Ecclesiastes choreographs with finesse. The Preacher's reflections encourage an embrace of the present moment, urging us to find joy in the simplest of life's treasures. "There is nothing better for a man, than that he should eat and drink, and that he should make his soul enjoy good in his labour" (Ecclesiastes 2:24). This acknowledgment of life's simple pleasures speaks to a universal truth: contentment can be found in the gratitude of daily blessings, a message as relevant today as it was in antiquity.

In this exploration of existential themes, Ecclesiastes invites its readers to engage in a profound philosophical inquiry—a search for purpose that transcends the boundaries of time and culture. The book's narrative is more than personal introspection; it's a communal invitation to question, reflect, and ultimately find peace in the ambiguity of life. As we navigate our own searches for meaning, guided by Ecclesiastes, we are encouraged to cultivate wisdom by embracing life's uncertainties, trusting in the divine sovereignty that orchestrates existence beyond our understanding.

The concluding chapters of Ecclesiastes steer towards an epiphany of sorts. The Preacher acknowledges that while human endeavors are fraught with vanity, there lies a simple truth: compliance with divine will is paramount. "Let us hear the conclusion of the whole matter: Fear God, and keep his commandments: for this is the whole duty of man" (Ecclesiastes 12:13). In this exhortation, Ecclesiastes encapsulates a timeless message, directing the faithful towards a life anchored in reverence and obedience, echoing through the corridors of biblical history into our contemporary search for purpose.

This profound reverence for divine wisdom not only addresses the futility presented earlier but also calls each believer to a higher understanding. It's an ultimate guide pointing toward spiritual enlightenment that can provide peace even amidst life's enigmas. The value in Ecclesiastes' teachings lies not in its answers but in the questions it compels us to wrestle with—questions that deepen our faith and enrich our understanding of what it means to live purposefully under the watchful eye of the Eternal.

For new believers and seasoned scholars alike, Ecclesiastes stands as both a puzzle and a guide—challenging, yet profoundly enlightening. It calls on us to abandon the pursuit of earthly vanities for transient enjoyment and to instead explore the depth of a life committed to spiritual reality. Within its verses lies a beacon, guiding those seeking knowledge through the complexities of human existence toward the illuminating embrace of divine wisdom.

Chapter 7:
The Influence of the Babylonian Exile

The Babylonian Exile is often seen as a pivotal event that profoundly shaped the course of Israelite history, culture, and theology. This period of displacement and adversity forced the Israelites to reflect deeply on their identity and covenant relationship with God. Stripped away from their homeland, they adapted by innovating religious practices and preserving their traditions, leading to a more defined sense of communal and spiritual identity. It was during this exile that synagogues emerged as centers for worship and communal life, laying the groundwork for Jewish religious practice. The longing for return and restoration echoed powerfully through their prophetic literature, as captured in the lamentations and hope of the Psalms. "By the rivers of Babylon, there we sat down, yea, we wept, when we remembered Zion" (Psalms 137:1), stands as a haunting testament to their yearning and resilience. The exile thus served not merely as a period of loss but as a crucible for renewal, forging a strengthened communal faith that would endure and evolve, even as they eventually returned to Judea, deeply impacting their theological reflections and future trajectories. Through these challenges, the Israelites' understanding of God and His promises reached new depths, providing a testament to the strength of faith under duress and the enduring hope for renewal even in the darkest of times.

Life in Exile

The Babylonian Exile, a period of profound disruption and transformation, serves as a powerful testament to human resilience and divine purpose. Living in exile was not merely a geographical dislocation but an existential recalibration. The Hebrew people found themselves torn from the familiar landscapes of Judah, facing the daunting task of redefining their identity under foreign skies. Yet, it was in the soil of adversity that the seeds of renewal were sown, for in their displacement, new expressions of faith and community emerged.

Babylon, a city of grandeur and complexity, challenged every familiar aspect of the Israelites' existence. The exiles had to navigate the cultural tapestry of a society vastly different from their own. Amid Babylon's towering ziggurats and bustling bazaars, they encountered an empire rich in diversity and steeped in idolatry. The prophet Ezekiel's visions, vivid and strange, encapsulate this duality of desolation and divine revelation: "As I was among the captives by the river of Chebar, that the heavens were opened, and I saw visions of God" (Ezekiel 1:1). Such experiences reflect a community grappling with maintaining their faith in a world that seemed to overshadow it.

Amidst the Babylonian splendor, the exiles confronted an identity crisis. How could they sing the Lord's song in a strange land? Yet, their response was not one of despair but of adaptation. The synthesis of lament and hope found in the Psalms reveals their profound ability to hold onto their covenant identity. "By the rivers of Babylon, there we sat down, yea, we wept, when we remembered Zion" (Psalms 137:1). Their tears watered the roots of a faith that would ultimately transcend geographical boundaries.

In the fertile atmosphere of Babylon, where cultural exchange was inevitable, the exiles found themselves in a crucible of transformation. Encountering Babylonian wisdom and learning, they did not shun it but positioned themselves as discerning recipients. It was a dynamic interplay of holding the sacred tradition while engaging with new knowledge. Daniel, a figure of unwavering faith, embodies this balance. Submerged in Babylonian culture, yet he remained committed to his God, becoming a beacon of integrity and insight.

As the exiles grappled with their new circumstances, significant theological developments occurred, reshaping their understanding of God and covenant. With the temple in ruins, the very heart of their worship rituals was inaccessible. Yet, absence birthed innovation; the synagogue emerged as a focal point for community cohesion and spiritual life, fostering scriptural engagement and collective worship. This shift emphasized the believers' direct access to God, reinforcing a faith resilient to geographical and political changes.

The exile also hastened a broader theological reflection on suffering and divine justice, themes poignantly addressed by prophets like Jeremiah and Second Isaiah. This period nurtured a deeper grasp of monotheism, crystallizing the belief in a God whose sovereignty extended beyond Judah's borders. "I am the Lord, and there is none else," declares Isaiah (Isaiah 45:5), a proclamation of faith and identity amidst foreign dominion.

Furthermore, the exilic period invited a reimagining of the covenant relationship, focusing less on land and more on a heart-centered faith. This inward turn reflected a community learning to find their foundation not in physical territory but in a covenantal relationship with a world-governing God. The Babylonian Exile became a catalyst for codifying traditions and scriptures, ensuring their preservation and continuity for future generations.

The community's resilience also lay in their capacity to nurture hope and expectation. The writings during and after exile speak of a return, a restoration not just materially but spiritually. Prophetic visions of renewal, such as those found in Ezekiel's visions of Israel's future and Isaiah's prophecies of a servant who would bring justice, ignited a spark of eschatological anticipation. They believed in a God who "removeth kings, and setteth up kings" (Daniel 2:21), an assurance of divine orchestration over history.

The exile fostered a sense of unity and collective identity, knitting the people together in a tapestry of shared experience and hope. This was a unity forged not in prosperity but in the fiery trials of displacement. They emerged as a diasporic community, understanding that their identity was indelibly linked to their relationship with God and each other, a legacy that continues to shape the Jewish faith today.

In summary, exile was as much about internal landscapes as it was about external environments. The story of the Babylonian Exile is a narrative of transformation through trial, a testament that out of the crucible of suffering can emerge a renewed faith and identity. It challenges us to look beyond our present circumstances, reminding us that growth often comes from adversity, and divine purpose may transcend human understanding. "For my thoughts are not your thoughts, neither are your ways my ways, saith the Lord" (Isaiah 55:8). This enduring lesson from an ancient people speaks to the heart of all who journey through life's challenges, assured that even in exile, there is life, growth, and a future firmly held in divine hands.

Cultural and Religious Adaptations During Exile

As the Jewish people found themselves thrust into the unfamiliar landscapes of Babylon, they were compelled to undergo profound cultural and religious transformations. The Babylonian Exile, though a period of profound sorrow, paradoxically became a fertile ground for the evolution and fortification of Jewish identity. Cut off from the Temple, the cornerstone of their worship, the Israelites faced the daunting challenge of preserving their faith and traditions in an alien land. This separation from their spiritual epicenter necessitated innovation and adaptation, forging new pathways for worship and community cohesion.

During this epoch, religious leaders sought to reinterpret Jewish customs and laws in a way that maintained their essence yet was adaptable to the conditions of exile. The Torah, particularly, was emphasized as a vital, unifying element—a portable homeland of sorts. It became the center around which the exiled community gathered. "Thy word is a lamp unto my feet, and a light unto my path" (Psalms 119:105). In these words, the significance of the Torah as both a spiritual and cultural guide during this period is illuminated.

In the absence of the Temple, the synagogue's role grew from necessity, marking a significant shift in religious practice. This development emphasized communal prayer and study, providing Jews with a new way to express their faith collectively. Synagogue gatherings highlighted the strength of community over individualism, nurturing a shared identity even in the face of external pressures. It was within these sacred spaces that the Diaspora Judaism we recognize today began to form, emphasizing the adaptability and resilience of Jewish worship.

Additionally, prayer became a crucial mechanism for maintaining a connection with their homeland and with God. Without the ability to offer sacrifices, which were central to their religious practice, the exiles turned to prayer as an immediate, personal way to communicate with the Divine. The words of Daniel, who continued to pray towards Jerusalem three times a day even under the threat of persecution, embody this new tradition: "Now when Daniel knew that the writing was signed, he went into his house; and his windows being open in his chamber toward Jerusalem, he kneeled upon his knees three times a day, and prayed, and gave thanks before his God, as he did aforetime" (Daniel 6:10).

The experiences of exile challenged the foundations of Jewish theology and cosmology. They encountered the vibrant polytheism dominating Babylonian society, which forced introspection and reevaluation of their beliefs. The Hebrew God, Yahweh, was understood anew, emphasizing His sovereignty not just over Israel but as a universal deity. This theological evolution can be seen through the prophetic voices like Ezekiel, who reassured them of God's enduring presence: "And I will give them one heart, and I will put a new spirit within you; and I will take the stony heart out of their flesh, and will give them an heart of flesh" (Ezekiel 11:19).

Moreover, during this time, new literary forms flourished. The wisdom tradition, apocalyptic literature, and elaborate covenant theology took root as Jews grappled with suffering and divine justice. Literature such as Lamentations and certain Psalms reflect this period's emotional and spiritual struggles, providing a poignant narrative of mourning and hope. Such texts not only served to express their current predicament but also provided future generations with profound insights into human resilience and faith.

Engagement with Babylonian culture wasn't one-sided. While maintaining their distinct identity, the Jewish community also borrowed and adapted certain aspects of Babylonian life to enrich their own. This cultural symbiosis influenced everything from language to legal practices. For instance, Aramaic became a lingua franca within the community, facilitating a broader communication that would later influence significant portions of Jewish religious texts.

The exilic period reinforced a sense of chosen-ness and the Abrahamic covenant. The Jewish stories and traditions preserved during this era continued to emphasize themes of covenant and promise, weaving a narrative that saw their exile not as abandonment by God but a divinely orchestrated plan for ultimate restoration. This narrative found echoes in texts like Isaiah, where the promise of return signifies hope: "Thus saith the Lord the God of Israel... I have loved thee with an everlasting love: therefore with lovingkindness have I drawn thee" (Jeremiah 31:3).

The ramifications of these adaptations went beyond the confines of Babylon, setting a template for Jewish survivability throughout future diasporas. They cultivated a paradigm of cultural resilience—transforming adversity into a catalyst for group solidarity and religious introspection. Such adaptations underscored a universal truth: that the core of spiritual life transcends physical locality and human obstacles, anchored instead in the strength of community, faith, and divine relationship.

Finally, as the winds of history shifted, allowing for the reestablishment in their homeland, these cultural and religious adaptations would resonate long after the exile concluded. The exilic experience served as a legacy of spiritual endurance and evolving identity. In exile, the Jewish people discovered that the spirit of their faith was neither confined to the walls of the Temple nor limited by geographical borders, but soared above them, touching the everlasting truths found within every heart turned towards God. As they returned to their homeland, they carried with them lessons carved out of suffering, yet shining with the promises of hope and renewal—a testament to the unyielding spirit and adaptive grace of a people determined to never let go of their divine calling.

Chapter 8: Intertestamental Developments

In the rich tapestry woven between the Old and New Testaments, the intertestamental period stands as a bridge of historical and cultural evolution, ripe with transformations that set the stage for the coming of Christ. This era, often seen as a chasm of silence, is in fact a dynamic time of Hellenistic influence that left indelible marks on Jewish life and thought. The conquests of Alexander the Great spread Greek culture and language across the Near East, permeating daily life and religious practices. Consequently, Jews grappled with maintaining their distinct identity amidst this foreign wave, as reflected in the period's literature and the critical findings of the Dead Sea Scrolls. These ancient texts provide profound insights into the diversity of Jewish beliefs and practices, highlighting the fervent expectation of a Messiah and the longing for spiritual renewal. As Proverbs reminds us, "In all thy ways acknowledge him, and he shall direct thy paths" (Proverbs 3:6), and this time of transition underscored a journey of cultural and spiritual navigation that would dramatically shape the narratives and teachings found in the Gospels.

Hellenistic Influence on Jewish Culture

As we dive into the intertestamental period, a time rich with transformation and adaptation, we encounter the profound impact of Hellenistic culture on Jewish society. This era, between the Old and New Testament writings, marks a pivotal phase where the influence of Greek civilization seeped through the fabric of Jewish life, bringing about changes that would resonate throughout the centuries. The spread of Hellenism, inaugurated by the conquests of Alexander the Great in the late fourth century BCE, introduced new challenges and opportunities for identity, faith, and expression among the Jewish people.

Under the expanding umbrella of Hellenistic rule, the Jewish people found themselves navigating a complex socio-political landscape. The Hellenistic period was characterized by a blend of Greek art, language, philosophy, and governance, which permeated numerous aspects of daily life. In places like Alexandria and Antioch, cosmopolitan hubs emerged, becoming melting pots of ideas, traditions, and cultures. Here, the Jewish diaspora began to encounter Greek thought and customs more directly, leading to significant cultural exchanges and sometimes conflict.

One striking feature of Hellenistic influence was the prevalence of the Greek language, which became the lingua franca of the Eastern Mediterranean. For Jewish communities, this necessitated the translation of Hebrew scriptures into Greek, resulting in the creation of the Septuagint. This monumental translation was more than a linguistic endeavor; it was an essential bridge that expanded the reach of Jewish religious texts, making them accessible to a broader, non-Hebrew-speaking population. The Septuagint played a critical role in the dissemination of Jewish thought and theology to the wider Hellenistic world, setting the stage for later Christian writings.

Yet, the Hellenistic influence wasn't limited to language. Greek philosophical schools like Stoicism, Epicureanism, and the teachings of Aristotle and Plato began to intermingle with Jewish thought. Some Jewish thinkers found commonalities with Greek wisdom, recognizing a shared pursuit of truth, ethics, and the divine. Others, however, viewed these philosophies as potential threats to the purity of their religious traditions. This dichotomy sparked vibrant discussions and debates within Jewish communities about the nature of wisdom, piety, and the interpretation of sacred texts.

Architecturally, the Hellenistic period left its mark with the introduction of Greek styles in public buildings and even synagogues. The establishment of gymnasia and other public spaces reflected Greek customs and social activities. These institutions often became centers for cultural exchange, where athletics, philosophy, and the arts were accessible to communities, including Jews. However, such integration was not without tension. The gymnasium, in particular, became a symbol of cultural assimilation that some Jewish groups opposed vehemently, associating it with idolatry and immorality.

The adaptation to Hellenistic culture manifested in varying degrees across different Jewish sects. The Sadducees, often aligning with Hellenist rulers, embraced a degree of acculturation, while the Pharisees sought to maintain religious purity and strict adherence to Torah laws in the face of foreign influences. This divergence in responses highlights the complex internal dynamics within Judaism during this period. The cultural negotiations and sometimes conflicts set the groundwork for significant theological development, which would later influence early Christian thought.

On a more personal level, the Hellenistic period prompted Jews to re-evaluate their identity and belonging. This era encouraged questions of what it meant to be Jewish in a Hellenistic world. Issues of identity were not merely philosophical—they had real-world implications on marriage, religious practices, and community life. The Maccabean Revolt exemplifies this struggle against Hellenistic imposition and stands as a testament to the fierce commitment to preserving Jewish identity against external pressure (see "1 Maccabees" Apocrypha).

This interplay of cultures also had practical effects. The marketplace, as a point of convergence, saw the blending of goods, traditions, and social interactions that reflected a unique mingling of

Greek and Jewish lifestyles. Such interactions enriched the Jewish community, introducing new culinary practices, artistic expressions, and even clothing styles, while simultaneously challenging traditional norms and values.

The influence of Hellenistic culture on Jewish literary production cannot be understated. Jewish writings from this period, including apocalyptic literature like the "Book of Daniel," exhibit Hellenistic influence through their form, language, and themes. These works grappled with the tension of maintaining faith and identity amidst foreign domination and cultural integration, providing rich insights that continue to inspire and inform contemporary Scriptural interpretation.

In reflecting on the Hellenistic influence, we recognize a period of Jewish history marked by energetic dynamism and profound introspection. Like a breath of fresh air, the cross-cultural exchanges of this time invigorated Jewish intellectual and spiritual life, pushing boundaries while crystallizing core tenets of faith. In recognizing the resilience and adaptability exhibited during this period, modern readers are inspired to appreciate the enduring legacy of this cultural encounter in shaping not only Jewish tradition but also the foundational texts of Christianity.

The dance of tradition and transformation witnessed in the Hellenistic period invites us to a deeper understanding of how external influences can both challenge and enrich faith. As the New Testament epistles would later echo this dynamic interplay, stating, "Prove all things; hold fast that which is good" (1 Thessalonians 5:21), we are reminded of the timeless power of discernment and the enduring strength of cultural and spiritual identity amidst change.

Significance of the Dead Sea Scrolls

In the grand tapestry of biblical history, few discoveries have generated as much fascination and debate as the Dead Sea Scrolls. Unearthed in a series of caves near Qumran between 1947 and 1956, these ancient texts offer an extraordinary glimpse into the intertestamental period, a time brimming with cultural, religious, and political shifts. But why do the Dead Sea Scrolls matter to those who seek to understand the intricate weave of the Scriptures? Their significance is multifaceted, touching on linguistic, theological, and historical dimensions, all of which illuminate the world just before the dawn of the New Testament era.

Linguistically, the scrolls provide invaluable insight into the languages of the period. Written in Hebrew, Aramaic, and Greek, they reflect the dynamic linguistic environment in which the Jewish people lived during the Second Temple period. This multilingual setting offers scholars a richer understanding of how language and culture intertwined, shining light on the semantic nuances present in the scriptural texts. Such nuances have profound implications for interpreting biblical passages accurately. The scrolls also include nearly complete versions of Old Testament books, important apocryphal writings, and other religious manuscripts that were once lost to history.

Consider the scrolls' contribution to biblical textual criticism. The scripts found at Qumran predate the previously oldest known Hebrew manuscripts by almost a thousand years, which allows for a direct comparison with later versions of the biblical text. This comparison helps scholars understand the transmission and preservation of Scripture over centuries. For example, when examining "Thy word is a lamp unto my feet, and a light unto my path" (Psalms 119:105), one gains a deeper appreciation for how this metaphor has been preserved across time and translations.

Theologically, the Dead Sea Scrolls open a window into the diverse religious thought that characterized this period. The scrolls reflect a community deeply concerned with purity, eschatology, and messianic expectations. These texts include the Community Rule, which outlines the beliefs and practices of the sect often associated with the Essenes. The insights gained from these writings allow readers to draw connections between the varied Jewish sects of the time and the teachings of Jesus and the early Christian movement, enriching the reader's grasp of the Gospels' cultural milieu.

The Messianic expectations found in the scrolls provide a particularly fascinating standpoint for interpreting messianic prophecies in the Scriptures. An environment of anticipation is palpable in "For unto us a child is born, unto us a son is given..." (Isaiah 9:6), which takes on deeper layers when viewed alongside Qumran documents expressing imminent hope for a coming deliverer. Understanding these expectations frames a backdrop for Jesus' ministry and the early Church's message, emphasizing how radical and transformative Jesus' teachings would have been in such a context.

Historically, the scrolls serve as a bridge between the Old and New Testament worlds. Embedded within the narratives are hints of how Judaism was practiced and evolved during times of great upheaval and change, especially under Hellenistic and Roman influences. This historical snapshot is pivotal for readers trying to trace the trajectory of Jewish thoughts and traditions as they transitioned into and eventually diverged into rabbinic Judaism and Christianity.

It's intriguing to consider how the societal dynamics echoed in these scrolls influenced the formation of the early church. As such, they elucidate themes of community, law, and salvation that resonate with the teachings of the Apostles. The communal lifestyle idealized in Acts, for instance, finds earlier reflections in the shared property and collective devotion seen at Qumran, painting a broader picture of how early Christian communities might have evolved.

Additionally, the scrolls provide a vibrant canvas of daily life, law, and morality, fleshing out the austere wilderness existence of the Qumran community against the backdrop of evolving Judean society. This backdrop parallels Proverbs' pragmatic insights into human behavior and Ecclesiastes' contemplations on life's meaning. Such texts provoke readers to consider broader biblical themes within the context of historical realities, offering clarity and depth that invigorate faith and understanding.

What the Dead Sea Scrolls continuously impress upon us is the vitality and diversity within ancient Judaism—an intricate tapestry from which early Christianity sprang forth. They challenge us to reflect on the dynamic interplay between faith and culture, inspiring renewed perspective and appreciation for the enduring impact of these ancient manuscripts on our spiritual journey today.

So, as we delve into the complexities and beauty of the Scriptures, may we remember the lessons and insights offered by these timeworn scrolls. We're reminded that history, language, and theology intermingle in a rich dialogue—a dialogue that beckons us to listen deeply and to seek paths of understanding through these sacred texts. In echoing the exhortation to "study to shew thyself approved unto God" (2 Timothy 2:15), let the knowledge of the Dead Sea Scrolls embolden you in your pursuit of spiritual wisdom and enlightenment.

Chapter 9: The Cultural Background of the Gospels

In weaving through the intricate tapestry of the Gospels, it's essential to grasp the nuanced cultural backdrop that shaped every parable, teaching, and miracle recorded within these sacred texts. The dynamic landscape of first-century Judea was a complex amalgam of Jewish traditions and Roman influence—a world where societal structures dictated daily life and religious observances intertwined with civic duties. As we delve into this cultural milieu, consider the Pharisees, Sadducees, and Essenes, each embodying distinct facets of Jewish religious life, while Roman governance imposed a pervasive political presence. Understanding this dual influence is pivotal, for it situates the teachings of Jesus within a context of resistance and renewal, where His message of love and redemption echoed against a backdrop of oppression and longing for spiritual liberation. "Render therefore unto Caesar the things which are Caesar's; and unto God the things that are God's" (Matthew 22:21) captures the delicate balance Jesus advocated in navigating these overlapping worlds. Thus, the eternal truths of the Gospels gain profound clarity when viewed through the lens of the cultural currents and historical intricacies that enveloped them. Each interaction, each sermon, emerges with resounding significance, urging us to not only read the words but to feel the urgency and hope they inspired in a people yearning for the profound embrace of divine truth.

Jewish Life in the First Century

In the vibrant tapestry of first-century Jewish life, one uncovers a world rich with tradition and expectation, a community living at the crossroads of hope and occupation. Society was deeply rooted in religious observance, with the Temple in Jerusalem standing as the center of worship and a symbol of national identity. Synagogues dotted the landscape, serving as focal points for instruction and communal gatherings. Amid Roman rule, Jewish cultural and legal practices coexisted with the complexities of external influence, frequently leading to tension but also adaptation. The Pharisees, Sadducees, Essenes, and Zealots represented distinct religious and political movements, each vying to interpret the Torah's significance. While some, like the Pharisees, emphasized strict adherence to law and oral traditions ("Matthew 23:3"), others, such as the Zealots, harbored revolutionary zeal. Embedded in this milieu, the teachings of Jesus offered radical insights into mercy and justice, resonating with those yearning for spiritual renewal. Understanding this dynamic culture provides profound insights into how the Jewish people navigated their lives in anticipation of the Messiah and illuminates the profound backdrop against which the Gospels unfolded.

Societal Structures in Jesus' Time were a tapestry of complexity and tradition, woven through the lives of the Jewish people in the First Century. The nuances of daily life are best understood by examining the societal structures that framed Jesus' teachings and interactions. With this tapestry as the backdrop, we can gain deeper insight into the Gospels and the pivotal moments of storytelling that have shaped spiritual thought for millennia.

During Jesus' time, society was deeply hierarchical. This structure could be observed in social, religious, and family spheres. The Jewish people were organized into classes with clear distinctions. At the top of societal hierarchies were the priests and religious leaders. Below them were the Levites, who served in temple duties but did not possess the same authority as priests. Socially, the Pharisees and Sadducees wielded significant influence. The Pharisees emphasized strict adherence to the law and oral traditions, while the Sadducees were known for their control of the temple and collaboration with Roman authorities. Jesus often interacted with these groups, critiquing their practices and challenging the status quo, as illustrated in passages like: "Woe unto you, scribes and Pharisees, hypocrites! for ye are like unto whited sepulchres, which indeed appear beautiful outward, but are within full of dead men's bones, and of all uncleanness" (Matthew 23:27).

The family served as the core of societal structure. Family ties dictated social dynamics, economic relationships, and religious obligations. Within a household, the father held patriarchal authority, a system that extended to the larger kinship networks. This kinship often went beyond mere familial bonds, influencing legal and economic transactions. The emphasis on lineage and ancestry underscored the Jewish people's connection to their heritage. Genealogies were critical, as reflected in the Gospel of Matthew's detailed account of Jesus' lineage, which traces His descent from Abraham, highlighting both His Judaic roots and messianic significance: "The book of the generation of Jesus Christ, the son of David, the son of Abraham" (Matthew 1:1).

Amidst these structures, the everyday activities of Jewish life—marketplaces bustling with trade, the routine of synagogue attendance, and the cyclical observance of festivals and Sabbaths—served as the crux of cultural vitality. For instance, the role of the synagogue was multifaceted. Not only was it a place of worship, but it also functioned as a community center and school. Moreover, synagogues were often places of theological debate and teaching, showcasing Jesus' encounters with religious scholars who marveled at His understanding and answered them, as noted: "And it came to pass, that after three days they found him in the temple, sitting in the midst of the doctors, both hearing them, and asking them questions" (Luke 2:46).

The Roman occupation added another layer of complexity to these structures. Under Roman rule, the Jewish people faced political oppression and heavy taxation, fundamentally affecting social interactions. Tax collectors, often despised for their role in enforcing Roman policies, are portrayed in the Gospels as outcasts. Yet, Jesus' revolutionary teachings invited them into His fellowship, offering grace and sparking change: "And as Jesus passed forth from thence, he saw a man, named Matthew, sitting at the receipt of custom: and he saith unto him, Follow me. And he arose, and followed him" (Matthew 9:9). The Roman presence also influenced the infrastructure and governance of Judea, shaping the environment in which Jesus and His disciples carried out their ministry.

The mounting pressure from Roman rule was met with a burgeoning hope for liberation and fulfillment of prophetic promises. Messianic expectations were heightened, yearning for a deliverer to break the shackles of oppression. Amid these expectations, Jesus' mission was both challenging and clarifying. His deliberate acts and parables shifted focus from an earthly kingdom to one rooted in spiritual renewal. Jesus' discourse on societal values was radical and transformative, urging a shift from external adherence to an inner transformation: "Blessed are the pure in heart: for they shall see God" (Matthew 5:8).

In the realm of education, teaching extended beyond formal structures. Oral tradition was the primary method of learning, pivotal for the transmission of laws, stories, and community identity. As demonstrated in the accounts of His followers, Jesus utilized parables—earthly stories with heavenly meaning—as a means to communicate profound truths to the masses. The reliance on oral traditions and parables fostered a sense of continuity and connection across generations, encouraging followers to grasp the essence of His teachings.

The era was also marked by a diversity of cultural and theological schools of thought. The Essenes, a separatist group, sought to live in purity and withdrew from urban centers. The Zealots, contrastingly, were driven by the belief that only through active resistance could the Jewish people free themselves from Roman rule. Each group presented a different approach to faith and resistance, laying a variety of cultural and social undercurrents that Jesus navigated in His ministry. His ability to bring diverse groups together under a common message of love and salvation broke down barriers, offering a vision of the Kingdom of God open to all: "And this gospel of the kingdom shall be preached in all the world for a witness unto all nations; and then shall the end come" (Matthew 24:14).

Family, faith, and societal order intertwined to create a unique tapestry in which Jesus ministered. Understanding these structures enriches our reading of the Gospel narratives, illuminating how they shape His teachings and their lasting implications. As we explore these societal dimensions, we can appreciate the radical nature of His message, which transcended the limitations of His time to resonate with timeless truth and wisdom.

Roman Impact on Judea

The Roman Empire's imprint on Judea was profound, shaping its cultural, political, and social landscape in ways that resonate throughout the Gospels. As we dive into this critical influence, we must remember that understanding the Roman occupation isn't just about grasping historical events; it's about seeing how these shaped the spiritual and daily lives of the people during Jesus' time.

Imagine Judea, a land of ancient promise, now under the heavy yoke of Roman rule. The mighty empire, known for its grand architecture and military might, did not just conquer lands— it wielded influence over the very fabric of society. Roman governance fundamentally altered Judean life, instigating changes that affected everything from local governance to religious practices. The presence of Roman officials like Pontius Pilate, mentioned explicitly in scripture, further illuminates this dynamic: "And Pilate gave sentence that it should be as they required" (Luke 23:24). Such narratives within the Gospels highlight the complex power dynamics at play.

One of the Romans' most apparent impacts was on the local governance system. The Sanhedrin, the assembly of Jewish leaders responsible for religious and civil matters, operated under the watchful eyes of Roman authorities. This compromise of autonomy was more than administrative. It created a palpable tension between Jewish leaders striving to maintain traditions and Roman officials imposing their will. The people's frustration is palpable when juxtaposed with the grace and revolution that Jesus preached, such as when he declared, "Render therefore unto Caesar the things which are Caesar's; and unto God the things that are God's" (Matthew 22:21). This balance between earthly and divine loyalties continues to inspire biblical interpretation today.

Economically, the Romans brought a mix of prosperity and oppression. Their infrastructure investments, notably in roads and cities like Caesarea Maritima, improved trade and communication, potentially broadening Israelites' horizons. Yet, these advancements came with hefty taxes and ... exploitation. Consider the tax collectors in the Gospels, often viewed with disdain by the Judean populace. Their role, as agents of the Roman Empire, reflects the burdensome tax system that the locals endured: "And when Jesus came to the place, he looked up, and saw him, and said unto him, Zacchaeus, make haste, and come down; for to day I must abide at thy house" (Luke 19:5).

This glimpse into Zacchaeus's life helps exemplify the personal struggles amidst larger economic forces.

The Roman cultural influence merged with Jewish tradition, creating a unique societal blend. Roman culture, known for its pantheon of deities, public spectacles, and philosophical schools, contrasted sharply with Jewish monotheism and religious life. This juxtaposition spurred on movements such as the Zealots, who fervently opposed Roman control, even inviting violent confrontations. Yet, the complexities of cultural integration weren't solely defined by conflict. Roman theaters, for instance, introduced new entertainment forms. The Roman world brought its version of peace, or <u>Pax Romana</u>, which, despite its coercions, offered some stability and connectedness in the broader Mediterranean world.

Religiously, the intersection of Roman beliefs and Jewish faith forged both friction and fusion. Roman religious tolerance permitted Judaism to practice relatively freely, but the empire's pantheon asserted pervasive pressure. Conflict arose over idolatry, intensified when Roman emperors demanded divine honors. The Gospels convey how this cultural interplay colored Jesus' ministry. Jesus' interactions often revealed the tension between the Kingdom of God and earthly kingdoms, urging a spiritual allegiance that transcended political boundaries: "My kingdom is not of this world: if my kingdom were of this world, then would my servants fight, that I should not be delivered to the Jews: but now is my kingdom not from hence" (John 18:36).

Then there's the language and literature exchange. Latin, alongside Greek, began seeping into the Judean vernacular. This linguistic flux facilitated the dissemination of the Gospel, connecting Jesus' teachings across cultural lines and appealing to a diverse audience. The ability to communicate across boundaries was pivotal in spreading the Christian message, echoing the Pentecost miracle: "And they were all filled with the Holy Ghost, and began to speak with other tongues, as the Spirit gave them utterance" (Acts 2:4). Understanding the multilingual environment further deepens our grasp of how these texts resonated far and wide.

Roman law imbued Judea with a structured judicial system that directly affected the trial and crucifixion of Jesus. The notorious cross, a Roman instrument of execution reserved for the vilest criminals, became the symbol of Christian faith through Christ's sacrificial death. This legal framework, emphasizing order and efficiency, facilitated Jesus' trial under Pontius Pilate, where political expediency prevailed over justice: "Then delivered he him therefore unto them to be crucified. And they took Jesus, and led him away" (John 19:16). This legal backdrop highlights the harsh realities of Roman rule while underscoring divine redemption.

The Roman impact on Judea persists as a testament to the adaptability and resilience of spiritual traditions under foreign dominion. It's about more than political and military occupation; it's an enduring lesson on how culture and faith intersect, forging paths of transformation and hope. As readers explore these dynamics, may they find inspiration in understanding how ancient struggles for identity, cultural negotiation, and spiritual fidelity have shaped the paths of faith over centuries.

Chapter 10:
Acts and the Early Church

As the curtain rises on the Acts of the Apostles, we witness the transformative journey of a nascent faith spreading through the arteries of the ancient world. This vibrant narrative, illuminated by the guidance of the Holy Spirit, showcases the early church's resilience and expansive spirit across diverse cultural terrains. Amidst trials and triumphs, Acts reveals the zealous commitment of disciples like Peter and Paul, who navigated the intricate mosaic of Greco-Roman society, extending the reach of Christianity far beyond Judea. With articulate sermons and miraculous deeds, these pioneers laid theological foundations that still resonate: the promise of salvation and the unity of believers in Christ's love. Witness Peter's bold declaration on the day of Pentecost: "Repent, and be baptized every one of you in the name of Jesus Christ for the remission of sins, and ye shall receive the gift of the Holy Ghost" (Acts 2:38). This episode not only spurred a cultural expansion but invited a diverse multitude to embrace a life transformed by the Spirit. Acts serves as a timeless testament to the power of faith-driven action, inspiring us to envision the boundless possibilities of a unified community, anchored in compassion and driven by a gospel that transcends cultural and geographical boundaries.

Cultural Expansion of Christianity

The Book of Acts vividly captures the dynamic spread of Christianity through the tapestry of the Greco-Roman world, a true testament to faith's power to transcend cultural boundaries. With Jerusalem as the nascent church's starting point, the message of Jesus swiftly moved into the heart of diverse cities and communities, challenging both societal norms and ingrained beliefs. As eternal truths resonated with seekers and skeptics alike, early followers harnessed the infrastructure and networks provided by the expansive Roman Empire. Apostles like Paul emerged as pivotal figures, adapting their approach to various cultures and perspectives; he famously reasoned with philosophers in Athens, declaring the identity of the "unknown god" (Acts 17:23). This era marked not just geographic growth but also a profound cultural exchange, as the Gospel harmonized with and sometimes clashed against prevailing traditions. The early church's endeavors remind us of an unstoppable force—a movement guided by the Holy Spirit to establish communities rooted in love, service, and profound spiritual transformation. Such narratives inspire modern readers to see how boundless faith can not only unite but also ignite change across the barriers of language and lands.

Spread Through Greco-Roman Society As the teachings of Christ began to ripple outward from Jerusalem, the nascent Christian movement navigated the dynamic and multifaceted landscape of Greco-Roman society. This period of remarkable growth saw the faith taking root in a world rich with cultural diversity, philosophical interest, and imperial complexity. But what made the Greco-Roman world such fertile ground for the spread of Christianity? It wasn't just a matter of historical inevitability but a convergence of factors that fueled the faith's expansion.

The Apostles, particularly Paul, ventured into a vibrant tapestry of cities across the Roman Empire—each with its own character, challenges, and opportunities. From Corinth to Rome, these urban centers were bustling hubs of commerce, cultural exchange, and philosophical debate. Acts 17:22-31 provides a vivid instance of this engagement during Paul's visit to Athens, where he conversed with Epicurean and Stoic philosophers about the "unknown god" and proclaimed the message of Christ's resurrection (Acts 17:23). These meaningful dialogues in the agora—the public square—allowed Christianity to engage directly with prevailing worldviews, offering a fresh paradigm grounded in the narrative of Jesus Christ.

The nature of Greco-Roman society also played a crucial role in Christianity's spread. The empire's extensive network of roads facilitated relatively swift travel, uniting distant provinces and making it feasible for messengers like Paul and other evangelists to traverse regions populated by diverse groups. As recorded in Romans 1:8, the faith of believers was "spoken of throughout the whole world" (Romans 1:8), a testament to how these roads became conduits for spiritual seeds to be planted and nurtured across varied terrains.

The linguistic unity offered by Koine Greek served as a bridge across cultures, easing communication and allowing the Christian message to transcend local dialects and reach a broader audience. This shared language was not just a medium but a vehicle for theological depth and philosophical engagement. As new converts came to understand and interpret their faith, this lingua franca enabled a scholarly exchange that enriched the church's doctrine and practice, laying the groundwork for theological discussions that would flourish in later centuries.

Moreover, the prevalent philosophical curiosity and religious pluralism were intriguing aspects of Greco-Roman culture. Into this setting of multiple gods and diverse beliefs came the compelling narrative of Jesus Christ—a singular divine revelation that proposed both an intimate relationship with God and a communal ethos based on love and service. As noted in the book of Galatians, "there is neither Jew nor Greek, there is neither bond nor free, there is neither male nor female: for ye are all one in Christ Jesus" (Galatians 3:28). Such teachings were revolutionary, transcending societal norms and galvanizing new communities built on principles of equality and compassion.

Interestingly, the Roman world's social conditions also facilitated the faith's appeal. The urban chaos, marked by class disparities and existential struggles, created a yearning for hope and solidarity that the Christian community offered. The mutual care and support among Christians starkly contrasted with the often impersonal and hierarchical structures of Roman society. Acts 2:44-47 illustrates how believers "had all things common," and this radical communal living made a profound impact on observers drawn by the transformative power of love and charity (Acts 2:44-47).

Yet, this proliferation was not without resistance and persecution. Early Christians often found themselves at odds with the Roman imperial cult and local religious practices. The refusal to worship the emperor or participate in pagan rituals branded followers of Christ as subverters of social order. In these trying circumstances, the perseverance of believers through trials and tribulations became a narrative of resilience and divine purpose, echoing Peter's exhortation to endure suffering as a testament to their faith (1 Peter 4:12-16).

That early Christians thrived under these challenges speaks volumes about their conviction and commitment to live out a faith defined by love, joy, and peace—the very fruits of the Spirit as outlined in Galatians 5:22-23. Their lives became a living testimony that attracted numerous individuals, fascinated by how Christianity delivered on its promises of hope and life transformation.

The cultural expansion of Christianity through the Greco-Roman society also rested on strategic conversions and the establishment of house churches, which were both intimate and meaningful. These gatherings, which took place in homes, allowed for personal discipleship and community growth. The decentralized nature of these early gatherings contributed to the faith's resilience and adaptability amid a vast and varied empire, allowing the movement to flourish despite external pressures.

In examining this dynamic spread, it's clear that Christianity's roots in the Greco-Roman world were not simply sown but meticulously cultivated. As the Christian message continued its journey across lands and peoples, it carried with it a transformative power—one that would not just survive the annals of history but shape the cultural and spiritual landscapes of the world for centuries to come. In this journey of faith crossing frontiers, we witness an incredible story of how divine providence interlaces with human history to enact profound change, speaking even today to hearts seeking belonging and truth beyond borders.

Theological Foundations in Acts

The book of Acts, a cornerstone of the New Testament, unveils the unfolding of early Christianity with a raw, transformative power. It serves as a theological bridge from the life of Jesus to the early church's formation. Through its vivid narrative, Acts encapsulates the vibrancy and authenticity of a movement rooted deeply in the teachings of Christ and empowered by the Holy Spirit. This section delves into the intricate tapestry of theological concepts presented within Acts, offering a profound insight into the early apostolic message that continues to echo throughout Christianity today.

The central theological theme in Acts is the proclamation of Jesus as the risen Messiah, the cornerstone of salvation. His resurrection is not merely a historical event but a transformative reality that continued to redefine the community's understanding of life and death. "Whom God hath raised up, having loosed the pains of death: because it was not possible that he should be holden of it" (Acts 2:24). This powerful assertion, delivered by Peter at Pentecost, underscores the resurrection as the nucleus of Christian faith, the axis around which the early church revolved.

Another fundamental aspect of Acts is the pervasive influence of the Holy Spirit. The Spirit's indwelling presence marks a new era for believers, empowering them to bear witness to Christ across diverse cultures and geographies. The Pentecost event, where the Holy Spirit descends on the apostles, is emblematic of this divine empowerment. "And they were all filled with the Holy Ghost, and began to speak with other tongues, as the Spirit gave them utterance" (Acts 2:4). This moment signifies the universal reach of the Christian message and the eradication of language as a barrier to spreading the gospel.

Moreover, Acts presents a compelling narrative of God's inclusivity. The theological underpinnings of divine acceptance are apparent in the bold admission of Gentiles into the early Christian fold. Peter's vision and subsequent interactions with Cornelius serve as a pivotal point. The revelation is clear: "Of a truth I perceive that God is no respecter of persons: But in every nation he that feareth him, and worketh righteousness, is accepted with him" (Acts 10:34-35). This profound inclusiveness challenged existing cultural norms, prompting the church to transcend its Jewish roots and embrace a global community.

The missional aspect of Acts is undeniable, embodying a call to witness and evangelize that resounds with urgency and passion. Paul's missionary journeys epitomize this call, reflecting a fervent determination to disseminate the gospel message despite adversity. At the heart of Acts lies the Great Commission, underscoring the theological belief that the kingdom of God knows no geographical boundaries. "But ye shall receive power, after that the Holy Ghost is come upon you: and ye shall be witnesses unto me both in Jerusalem, and in all Judaea, and in Samaria, and unto the uttermost part of the earth" (Acts 1:8). This mandate propelled the nascent church outward, reaching into the heart of the Roman Empire.

Additionally, the book of Acts emphasizes the formation of a new community centered on teachings, fellowship, and breaking of bread. The early church in Jerusalem is depicted as a vibrant community devoted to the apostles' doctrine and to communal living. "And they continued stedfastly in the apostles' doctrine and fellowship, and in breaking of bread, and in prayers" (Acts 2:42). This blueprint for communal faith life extends beyond ritual; it is an expression of deep solidarity and mutual care, revealing the theological significance of community in the Christian life.

Acts also articulates a theology of suffering and perseverance. The early church's experience of persecution is not presented as a mere historical fact but as a theological lens through which the power of God is seen at work even in adversity. Stephen's martyrdom, for example, is a testament to unwavering faith and forgiveness that confounds earthly power with divine love. "Lord, lay not this sin to their charge" (Acts 7:60). This ability to emulate Christ even in the face of death encapsulates the profound spiritual resilience of the Christian community.

Another core theological theme is the tension between law and grace. As the church expands to include Gentiles, questions of adherence to Mosaic Law surface, leading to the Jerusalem Council. This landmark moment in Acts highlights a theological pivot towards grace as the heart of salvation. "But we believe that through the grace of the Lord Jesus Christ we shall be saved, even as they" (Acts 15:11). This declaration emphasizes the sufficiency of Christ's sacrifice and sets a precedent for understanding Christian identity apart from the law.

The theological implications of Acts do not rest solely within the narrative itself but reverberate throughout Christian theology and practice. The book challenges believers to consider their role in God's ongoing narrative of redemption and compels them to live with conviction, courage, and compassion. Acts invites readers to reflect on the transformative power of faith, urging a deeper engagement with the foundational truths that have shaped Christianity for centuries.

Ultimately, the theological foundations in Acts articulate a vision of a church that is dynamically alive, embodying the teachings of Jesus in a broken world. This vision calls us to embody the same courage, grace, and unity demonstrated by the early apostles. The narrative of Acts, though ancient, speaks to the contemporary Christian experience, urging believers to embrace their role as bearers of hope and love in an ever-changing world. As readers explore this transformative text, they are reminded that the story of Acts is not merely a historical account, but an ongoing mission that calls each individual to participate in God's redemptive plan for humanity.

Chapter 11: Pauline Epistles and Cultural Engagement

As we delve into the Pauline Epistles, the rich tapestry of cultural engagement comes to the forefront. The Apostle Paul, navigating the intricate pathways of Jewish and Greco-Roman worlds, unveils a revolutionary approach to faith and society. His letters, brimming with passionate discourse, reveal his adeptness at weaving cultural threads into the fabric of divine truth, making them both relevant and timeless. By addressing audiences ranging from the devout cliques of Corinth to the philosophical minds in Athens, Paul's epistles are masterpieces of contextual theology. He champions unity in diversity, as articulated in his plea, "There is neither Jew nor Greek, there is neither bond nor free, there is neither male nor female: for ye are all one in Christ Jesus" (Galatians 3:28). This profound insight transcends mere cultural exchange, calling for a revolutionary society rooted in love and equality. His teachings challenge believers to engage with the world thoughtfully, echoing through time as a beacon for cultural dialogue and transformation. The Pauline Epistles thus serve as a guide, inviting readers to explore the balance between maintaining one's roots and embracing the broader cultural narrative, urging a faith that is both profound and pragmatic.

Paul's Cultural Contexts

As we delve into Paul's epistles, we uncover a tapestry of cultural elements that weave through his writings, revealing the complex backdrop of his world. Paul was a man of diverse influences, traversing between Jewish traditions and Greco-Roman society, each leaving an indelible mark on his teachings. His ability to communicate the Gospel within these varied contexts was nothing short of extraordinary, as he crafted messages that resonated deeply with his audience. When Paul wrote, "To the Jews I became as a Jew, that I might gain the Jews" (1 Corinthians 9:20), he wasn't simply stating a strategy; he was embodying a profound commitment to cultural engagement. Through understanding Paul's cultural milieu, we gain insights into his fervent mission, rooted in love and wisdom, to bridge cultural divides and bring the transformative power of Christ's message to all corners of the earth. This understanding calls us to reflect on how we, too, can engage with our own diverse cultures with similar zeal and authenticity, carrying the torch of illumination in our time.

Jewish and Greco-Roman Influences As we delve into Paul's cultural contexts, one cannot overlook the profound tapestry of Jewish and Greco-Roman elements that interweave throughout his epistles. Paul, a man of dual heritage, straddled two worlds with remarkable ease. His Jewish roots were deeply ingrained, having been brought up in strict adherence to the Mosaic Law, while his Roman citizenship provided him with a unique vantage point to engage with the sprawling Greco-Roman society. This fusion of identities enriched his theological insights, giving rise to epistles that resonated with diverse audiences across the ancient world.

Understanding Paul requires a glimpse into his Jewish upbringing. Born Saul of Tarsus, he was a Pharisee, grounded in the traditions of his forefathers. His grasp of Jewish laws and customs wasn't merely academic; it was lived and deeply personal. When Paul argues for the continuity and fulfillment of Jewish expectations in Christ, such as in Romans 9-11, he's not just making a theological case; he's weaving his life's journey into the broader narrative of Israel. This intimate connection with his Jewish heritage shows how he viewed Jesus as the culmination of God's promise to Abraham and the patriarchs (Romans 4:13).

Yet, Paul's letters also reflect a sophisticated engagement with the Greco-Roman world. His use of rhetoric and philosophical concepts would feel at home in the public forums of Athens or the bustling marketplaces of Corinth. In Acts 17, we see him step into the Areopagus, deftly quoting Greek poets to relate the gospel to the philosophically curious minds of the day. His ability to pivot from Jewish genealogies to Greco-Roman ideals exhibits the skillful cultural translation that marks his epistles.

The wisdom of this approach is evident in how Paul addresses both Jewish and Gentile believers within the communities he nurtured. Take, for instance, his letter to the Galatians. Here, Paul navigates the tension between Jewish identity and the new faith in Jesus Christ. He challenges the necessity of circumcision, a core tenet of Jewish identity, by casting it in light of a new covenant, where faith and love prevail over law (Galatians 5:6). Yet, he doesn't dismiss the law entirely; instead, he reframes it, illustrating his nuanced understanding of Jewish tradition within the realm of a wider Greco-Roman discourse.

Moreover, Paul's letters often mirror the Greco-Roman literary structure, such as employing diatribe style in Romans to engage and refute potential objections. The manner in which he writes—introducing questions and then addressing them himself—engages readers and hearers of his letters, prompting them to reflect deeply on their faith and cultural identities. This technique was characteristically employed by philosophers of his time, a potent reminder that Paul was as comfortable amongst scrolls and synagogues as he was under colonnades and temples.

Consider also the philosophical underpinnings that colored his teachings. Paul famously incorporated the Hellenistic concept of the "logos" or the "word." In conveying the Christian message of reconciliation and divine wisdom, he spoke a language familiar to both Jews who revered the Torah and Greeks who contemplated the rational order of the cosmos. This synthesis of ideas facilitated the spread of Christianity beyond Judea, reaching into the very heart of Gentile philosophy and understanding.

Even the mention of sports metaphors, a common theme in Greco-Roman culture, found its way into Paul's letters. His references to running a race and striving for a prize (1 Corinthians 9:24) served as vivid imagery, easily grasped by recipients of his epistles who were steeped in the culture of athletic contest and glory. Such metaphors weren't merely ornamental; they were strategic, enabling Paul to connect deeply with his audience's lived experiences and aspirations.

Paul's ability to reconcile these two culturally rich traditions into a unified message of faith not only speaks to his intellectual versatility but also to his inspired mission. He becomes a bridge, not only between Jew and Gentile but also across human cultures, illustrating the gospel's transcendent reach. His letters became a testament to a new reality — one where identity was reimagined in Christ, surpassing ethnic, social, and cultural barriers.

In light of these influences, Paul's epistles beckon readers to reflect on the interplay between their cultural contexts and spiritual lives. His life and letters challenge us to see how our backgrounds and beliefs can be harmonized under the guidance of divine wisdom. Indeed, Paul's adept cultural engagement provides a template for contemporary cross-cultural dialogue, urging believers to integrate yet transcend their cultural identities in the pursuit of shared kingdom values.

As we navigate our own intricate cultural landscapes, Paul's example inspires us to recognize the divine opportunities embedded within our unique heritages. By embracing the richness of our backgrounds and engaging with those beyond our immediate contexts, we open ourselves to the boundless possibilities that faith presents. Like Paul, we're called to be both rooted and expansive, drawing from the wellspring of our traditions while casting a wider net toward a universal narrative of hope and salvation.

Key Themes in the Epistles

The apostle Paul's epistles stand as timeless instruction, offering wisdom, guidance, and profound insight into the nature of faith and the Christian journey. Yet, to truly grasp their significance, we must explore the key themes interwoven throughout his letters. These themes not only addressed the challenges of the early church but also resonate deeply within us today. They are foundational to understanding Paul's engagement with the culture of his time while laying principles that transcend the ages.

One of the most pervasive themes within Paul's writings is grace. To consider grace is to step into a realm of unmerited favor and transformative power that Paul argues is freely given to all believers through Jesus Christ. His declaration in Ephesians, "For by grace are ye saved through faith; and that not of yourselves: it is the gift of God" (Ephesians 2:8), echoes through the centuries, reminding us that our spiritual renewal and salvation do not come from our deeds but through divine grace. This radical concept challenged not just Jewish precepts of law but also the meritocratic ethos of Greco-Roman culture.

Faith, closely coupled with grace, emerges powerfully in Paul's epistles. In a world often dictated by sight and empirical evidence, Paul champions a life led by faith. He famously proclaims, "For we walk by faith, not by sight" (2 Corinthians 5:7). This commitment to faith as a lens through which reality can be interpreted serves as a call to believers to transcend physical limitations and embrace a spiritual life rooted in trust and conviction.

Another cornerstone of Paul's message is love, which he describes as the greatest of all virtues. His epistle to the Corinthians dedicates a chapter to its enduring beauty and indispensability, stating plainly, "And now abideth faith, hope, charity, these three; but the greatest of these is charity" (1 Corinthians 13:13). Here, love, or 'agape,' is depicted not merely as an emotion but as an active, enduring force, a divine attribute that both reflects and fulfills the law (Romans 13:10). This principle of love speaks to personal and communal transformation, challenging believers to embody love in action.

The theme of unity in the body of Christ is another focal point in Paul's letters. His assertion that "there is neither Jew nor Greek, there is neither bond nor free, there is neither male nor female: for ye are all one in Christ Jesus" (Galatians 3:28) was revolutionary, breaking down societal and cultural barriers. Paul encourages the church to view itself as a cohesive body, where diversity of gifts and backgrounds strengthens rather than divides. This message of unity was critical for the culturally diverse congregations of the early church and remains equally pertinent in our contemporary global society.

Paul's discussion of moral and ethical living intertwines throughout his epistles. He provides practical guidance on living out one's faith in the often conflicting mainstream culture. In his letter to the Romans, he instructs believers, "Be not conformed to this world: but be ye transformed by the renewing of your mind" (Romans 12:2). For Paul, the call to holiness is a transformative process that begins with the mind and heart, leading to actions aligned with divine will. His ethical teachings are not mere rules but are rooted in the love and righteousness of God, meant to inspire believers toward authentic living.

A theme with enduring relevance is the anticipation of Christ's return, the eschatological hope. Paul writes to the Thessalonians with urgency and assurance about the second coming of Jesus, encouraging them to live vigilantly and with hopeful expectancy: "For yourselves know perfectly that the day of the Lord so cometh as a thief in the night" (1 Thessalonians 5:2). This anticipation of the future reign shifts the believer's perspective on suffering, perseverance, and the transient nature of the present world.

Paul's discourse on spiritual warfare is another profound issue, drawing attention to the pervasive spiritual battles believers face. His meticulous outline of the "whole armour of God" in Ephesians serves as a tactical guide for spiritual resilience: "Put on the whole armour of God, that ye may be able to stand against the wiles of the devil" (Ephesians 6:11). Through this metaphor, Paul emphasizes the need for awareness, preparedness, and reliance on divine strength, rather than human means, to withstand spiritual adversities.

Finally, the theme of suffering and perseverance underlies much of Paul's writing. He frames suffering not as a sign of divine abandonment but as a means of spiritual growth and deeper communion with Christ. His own life is a testament to this theology, finding strength in weakness and contentment in adversity: "And he said unto me, My grace is sufficient for thee: for my strength is made perfect in weakness" (2 Corinthians 12:9). Through this lens, suffering is neither glorified nor minimized, but used to cultivate reliance on God and a steadfast spirit.

In exploring these themes, we encounter Paul not just as an apostle but as a bridge between cultures, as well as an artist of divine truth, shaping a narrative that speaks to the essence of Christian belief. His epistles invite believers to embark on a transformative journey, navigating the currents of culture while anchored in timeless truths. As we reflect on Paul's letters, may we allow these key themes to penetrate our hearts and minds, inspiring not only understanding but also action, drawing us closer to the heart of God.

Chapter 12: Revelation and Apocalyptic Literature

The Book of Revelation and its apocalyptic companions offer a vivid canvas of imagery and symbolism, drawing us into a domain where the seen and unseen realms entwine. In these texts, the veil between the earthly and the divine trembles, revealing a cosmic drama that has captivated minds and hearts for centuries. As we delve into this mysterious literature, we uncover a treasure trove of cultural and historical contexts that elucidate its enigmatic visions. The author of Revelation, traditionally identified as John, crafts a narrative rich with allusions to the Old Testament, evoking battle scenes, divine judgment, and eventual redemption, as found in passages like "Behold, he cometh with clouds" (Revelations 1:7). These apocalyptic writings were birthed in times of persecution and turmoil, weaving hope for the oppressed and projecting a future where justice prevails. Interpretation remains a venture fraught with challenge, requiring us to sift through layers of metaphorical language that tease the imagination while resisting simplistic explanation. By anchoring our study in cultural context, we gain insights into the hopes and fears of early Christians navigating a world that often stood against them, fueling their resilient faith in an unfolding divine plan.

Cultural and Historical Context of Revelation

Revelation, a book that has captivated and perplexed readers for centuries, emerges from a time and place steeped in profound cultural and historical significance. To fully grasp its message, it's essential first to understand the milieu in which it was composed. The author, traditionally recognized as John the Apostle, penned these visions during the latter part of the first century A.D. This period was marked by intense persecution and tumultuous change, circumstances that infused the text with urgency and fervor.

The Roman Empire cast a long shadow over the early Christian community, profoundly influencing the texture and tone of Revelation. Under the reigns of emperors like Nero and Domitian, Christians faced severe persecution, hunted as enemies of the state for their refusal to partake in the cult of emperor worship. This persecution was not only a physical oppression but also a psychological and spiritual battle, as believers were continually challenged to maintain their faith amidst adversity. This context of suffering is vividly depicted in the apocalyptic imagery of Revelation, where the forces of evil are portrayed as formidable but ultimately doomed to defeat.

While the specter of Rome looms large, it's crucial to consider the spiritual and theological climate of John's era. This was a time when apocalyptic literature was a popular genre among Jewish and early Christian writings. Works like the Book of Daniel and various intertestamental texts set a precedent for this style of storytelling. Apocalyptic literature often employs symbolic language to reveal divine truths hidden within current events, granting hope to the faithful that God is in control, even when circumstances suggest otherwise. Revelation stands firmly within this tradition, offering a cosmic vision that transcends human history and points to God's ultimate victory.

Jewish apocalyptic thoughts significantly influenced John, shaping the symbols and themes present throughout the text. Concepts like the battle between light and darkness, the final judgment, and the messianic reign are deeply rooted in Jewish theology. John's familiarity with Hebrew Scriptures allows him to weave these themes intricately, creating a rich tapestry that draws from the past to inform the present and future. When John writes of "the new heaven and a new earth" (Revelations 21:1), he echoes the prophetic visions of Isaiah, envisioning a redemptive transformation that fulfills ancient promises.

Moreover, the sociopolitical tension against the Roman Empire finds a distinct expression in Revelation. The symbolic language serves as a dual-purpose veil and weapon, concealing its subversive message from Roman authorities while encouraging Christians to remain steadfast in their faith. References to Babylon, the great harlot, and the beast each carry nuanced meanings that would have resonated with John's contemporaries, who saw in them the oppressive hand of Rome and its eventual downfall. These symbols are not just theological metaphors but are drawn from the cultural experiences of a people under siege.

The cultural exchanges and interactions within the Roman Empire also play a role in the shaping of Revelation's narrative. The early Christian community was not isolated but was influenced by the diverse tapestry of peoples and ideas that traversed the empire. Commerce, philosophy, and religious thought intermingled, creating a dynamic environment where ideas could evolve and spread rapidly. This cosmopolitan context informed the imagery of Revelation, where various elements reflect the myriad cultures within which the early Christian church found itself.

Economic pressures also contribute to the broader narrative, as Revelation dives into the societal and moral critiques of a world driven by greed and power. The condemnation of the mercantile Babylon illustrates a critique against the economic exploitation and moral decay of John's day. This criticism speaks directly to the experiences of communities struggling under imperial taxations and exploitative labor practices, amplifying the call for justice and righteousness found throughout the text.

Additionally, Revelation captures the spiritual dynamics of worship and devotion that were central to early Christian identity and practice. Against the backdrop of Roman imperial cultic practices, John instructs believers to worship only God, highlighting the spiritual resistance that characterized early Christian communities. The visions repeatedly steer readers towards a cosmic worship scene, where creation joins in eternal praise, providing a stark contrast to the earthly veneration of emperors and idols.

As one delves into Revelation, the cultural and historical context is not merely background information but is deeply intertwined with its theological message. Understanding the historical pressures and cultural influences not only enriches the text's interpretation but also illuminates its timeless relevance. This complex interplay serves as a powerful reminder of the endurance of faith across the ages, and how God's promises transcend the fleeting tribulations of human history.

Revelation beckons readers to participate in a visionary journey that defies temporal limitations. Its enduring message of hope and victory emanates from the resilience of a community that clung to divine promises in times of despair. Reflecting on its cultural and historical roots, we find inspiration in the realization that this message was forged in the crucible of human struggle and divine revelation. In understanding this context, the tapestry of symbols and visions in Revelation becomes a guide, offering insights into both ancient and current paradigms, and forever pointing towards the triumphant hope that is found in faith.

Interpretation Challenges and Cultural Insights

The Book of Revelation, with its vivid imagery and profound symbolism, offers a unique interpretative challenge, deeply entwined with the ancient cultural and historical contexts that birthed it. Understanding this apocalyptic literature requires diving into the cultural milieu of the first-century Mediterranean world, where Roman imperial power and local traditions clashed and converged. Imagery such as beasts, dragons, and the notorious number 666 reflect more than cryptic forebodings; they symbolically embody the socio-political tensions of that era. Revelation's layered narratives unlock the insights of divine justice and hope interwoven amid persecution, calling readers to discern deeper spiritual truths. These challenges are not merely academic exercises but invitations to explore what lies beneath the surface, motivating believers to find personal and communal resonances in the timeless struggle between darkness and light. John's vision, while complex, encourages us all to look beyond the apocalyptic to the assurance found in the Lamb that was slain, saying, "Behold, I come quickly" (Revelations 22:12). Engaging with Revelation through this lens heightens our appreciation of its messages, weaving together the historical, the prophetic, and the culturally profound.

Online Review request for This Book If you've found the exploration of "Interpretation Challenges and Cultural Insights" within apocalyptic literature enlightening, kindly consider sharing your thoughts through an online review to help others discover the profound revelations this book offers.

Conclusion

The journey through the pages of this book has endeavored to weave a tapestry that connects the intricate cultural, historical, and theological threads of biblical texts. We have ventured across centuries, exploring ancient worlds and deep-seated beliefs that have shaped how these sacred scriptures speak to the hearts and minds of readers today. As you close this chapter, may your understanding of the Bible's depth and richness be deepened, and may you find new ways to integrate its wisdom into your personal and spiritual journey.

Each chapter aimed to peel back layers, revealing the complex interplay of culture and faith that underlies the biblical narrative. As Paul once reflected, "For now we see through a glass, darkly" (1 Corinthians 13:12). We've tried to polish that glass a bit, offering clearer insights into texts that resonate through history and into the present. Whether you approached this text as a scholar or a seeker, our hope is that you've discovered how understanding the broader contexts of the scripture enriches its message.

The cultural contexts—whether Egyptian practices influencing Exodus or Greco-Roman customs in the New Testament—serve as a reminder that these texts were lived experiences. Each story, law, and prophecy served a purpose within its time and continues to brim with lessons for us today. The cultural landscapes these texts were born into are vibrant tapestries, offering us views from viewpoints we might not have initially considered. Consider the Genesis family structures or the societal shifts during the Babylonian Exile; they remind us that the settings of these stories matter just as much as the stories themselves.

The historical contexts remind us of the ebbs and flows of nations and empires that shaped and were shaped by their encounters with divine interaction. From the rise and fall of Israel's monarchy to the seismic shifts caused by the Babylonian Exile and the profound impact of Hellenistic cultures during intertestamental times—each period layered new dimensions to the spirituality and survival of God's people.

The book's pathway through the language of the scriptures—from the ancient tongues of Hebrew and Aramaic to Greek—also emphasizes the importance of translation's role in sustaining the Bible's message across cultures and eras. Every new translation effort echoes the apostles' Pentecostal moment where "every man heard them speak in his own language" (Acts 2:6). This ongoing miracle permits individuals from myriad backgrounds to experience the scriptures deeply and personally, ensuring its continued relevance and resonance.

Our exploration of Biblical wisdom literature reveals an ongoing conversation on human life's paradoxes and eternal quests for meaning. Whether resting in the pragmatic wisdom of Proverbs or the existential inquiries of Ecclesiastes, these texts serve as spiritual companions, reminding us that seeking God's truths is an ever-unfolding journey.

And consider the dynamic world of early Christianity's expansion chronicled in Acts. Through cultural engagement and theological grounding, the early church navigated its path in a largely Greco-Roman sphere, affirming that the essence of the Gospel transcends cultural boundaries. Paul's epistles continue to guide the faithful on how to live a life shaped by grace amidst prevailing cultural currents.

Lastly, as our journey concludes with apocalyptic literature and the Book of Revelation, we are reminded of the hope embedded within its symbolic visions. John's revelation remains a beacon for enduring hope and perseverance, underscoring the truth that despite cultural upheaval, divine promises hold firm: "Surely I come quickly" (Revelations 22:20). This anticipation of God's kingdom is a steadfast anchor amid life's storms.

As you leave this text, may you carry forward an enhanced appreciation of the Bible's profound interconnectedness with culture and history. Let this be a launching point enabling you to dive deeper into the Word, unearthing its boundless wisdom and transformative power. May it inspire you to not only understand these sacred texts more deeply but to live out their truths with renewed conviction and clarity.

In closing, be inspired by the timeless call to cross the threshold from understanding to embodiment. The scriptures, imbued with ancient wisdom, beckon us to find relevance and purpose in their pages, to live out a faith that is both informed and vibrant in today's world. May we continue to walk this path with courage and curiosity, enriched by the ever-present and transformative Word of God. Amen.

Appendix A: Appendix

As we close this exploration of biblical contexts, it's vital to recognize the transformative journey knowledge can spark within us. This appendix extends a bridge to further discovery, offering an array of resources for deepening one's understanding of the cultural and historical layers woven within the Scriptures. The Bible, timeless in its wisdom, serves as a wellspring of divine guidance—an ancient text waiting to unfold its mysteries in the heart of the earnest seeker. "For the wisdom of this world is foolishness with God" (1 Corinthians 3:19), reminding us that each step we take towards comprehending its message brings us closer to the essence of divine truth. Here, you will find tools designed to illuminate and expand your biblical studies, encouraging a pursuit of truth that resonates beyond the confines of time and place. Let these additional materials motivate a deeper engagement, aiding every student of the Bible, whether novice or sage, to uncover not only the Word's historical breadth but its profound impact on personal faith and spirituality. This pursuit leads into the realms of understanding that shine light upon life's greatest questions and challenges, fueling a transformation as vast as the stories within these sacred passages.

Additional Resources for Cultural and Historical Studies of the Bible

In our quest for a deeper understanding of the biblical texts, it's essential not only to delve into the scriptures themselves but also to harness a variety of resources that illuminate the rich cultural and historical tapestry of the Bible. These resources act as a bridge, allowing us to traverse time and space and view ancient worlds with fresh eyes and renewed minds.

The study of archaeology offers a tangible connection to the past, unearthing artifacts and remnants of civilizations that provide context to the biblical narrative. Discoveries such as the Dead Sea Scrolls have broadened our comprehension of Jewish life and thinking during the Second Temple period, a pivotal era that shaped the milieu of the New Testament (Matthew 5:18). Dive into works like "Biblical Archaeology: A Very Short Introduction" by Eric H. Cline, which succinctly explores these findings and their implications for biblical studies.

Linguistic studies also furnish invaluable insights. The original languages of the Bible, primarily Hebrew, Aramaic, and Greek, are the lenses through which the scriptures were first viewed and understood. Familiarizing oneself with linguistic tools can deepen appreciation of nuances often lost in translation. Resources such as "The Text of the New Testament: Its Transmission, Corruption, and Restoration" by Bruce Metzger serve as quintessential guides for anyone seeking to understand the New Testament's complex transmission history.

For a more cultural-centric exploration, consider exploring books like "The Cultural World of the Bible" by Victor H. Matthews. This work provides detailed discussions of the cultural customs and social practices prevalent during biblical times, offering context for events and teachings within Scripture. Understanding these cultural cues can transform our reading of passages like the parables of Jesus, whose messages were deeply rooted in the cultural settings of His audience (Luke 14:23).

Historical atlases are another treasure trove for biblical scholars. They map the geopolitical landscapes of biblical times, lending clarity to the movements and migrations that define so many of the sagas within the Bible. "The Baker Atlas of Christian History" provides detailed maps that chart the development and spread of Christian communities, offering visual context to the journeys in Acts and beyond.

Interaction with complementary religious texts, such as those found in the Apocrypha and Pseudepigrapha, can be eye-opening. These texts, though not canonical for all traditions, offer insights into the religious landscape of the intertestamental period and the diversity of thought within Judaism. "The New Oxford Annotated Bible with Apocrypha," known for its comprehensive annotations, is an excellent resource for those interested in these supplementary texts.

Finally, engaging with contemporary biblical scholarship via journals and online platforms ensures that one's study remains dynamic and current. Journals such as the "Journal of Biblical Literature" or the "Biblical Archaeology Review" publish cutting-edge research and discussion by scholars from various disciplines. These resources continually challenge and expand our understanding, reminding us that the study of the Bible is an ever-evolving journey.

While this list is by no means exhaustive, these resources can significantly enrich one's study of the Bible. They serve not only as tools for understanding but also as reminders of the vibrant and complex world from which the scriptures emerged. As you explore these additional resources, may you find your knowledge and faith deepened, your questions sharpened, and your spirits inspired to engage with the Word anew. The Bible invites us into a dialogue across the ages, where every exploration leads us closer to the heart of its eternal truth. "For whatsoever things were written aforetime were written for our learning, that we through patience and comfort of the scriptures might have hope" (Romans 15:4).

Printed in Great Britain
by Amazon